Anonymous

Pacific line guide to South America; containing information to travellers & shippers to ports on the east & west coasts of South America

Anonymous

Pacific line guide to South America; containing information to travellers & shippers to ports on the east & west coasts of South America

ISBN/EAN: 9783337208363

Printed in Europe, USA, Canada, Australia, Japan

Cover: Foto ©Andreas Hilbeck / pixelio.de

More available books at **www.hansebooks.com**

S. F. 8

THE PACIFIC STEAM NAVIGATION CO.

Incorporated Under Royal Charter 1840

—AND—

COMPAÑIA SUD=AMERICANA DE=VAPORES

San Francisco, Dec. 19, 1901.   In effect immediately.

First-Class Twin Screw Passenger Steamers

FROM

SAN FRANCISCO

TO

Mexico, Central America, Panama, Guayaquil, Callao, Valparaiso and all Ports on the East and West Coast of South America.

Each Steamer carries an experienced Surgeon. Prompt attention paid to **Written or Telegraphic Requests for Reservation** of State Rooms or Berths.

Cabin plans on exhibition, passage tickets for sale and all information at

Balfour Guthrie & Co.

General Agents

GEORGE SHARPE,
  MANAGER P. S. N. C.

HORACIO LYON,
  MANAGER C. S. A. DE V.

316 California St.

SAN FRANCISCO

The Pacific Steam Navigation Co. and
Compañía Sud=Americana de Vapores

Rates of Passage from San Francisco to Points on Pacific Coast, Payable in United States Gold Coin.
U. S. Revenue Stamp Additional.

Special Tariff Subject to Change Without Notice.

Miles from S. F.	SAN FRANCISCO TO		FIRST CLASS	DECK
1352	Mazatlan	Mexico	$ 45 00	$ 22 50
1476	San Blas	"	50 00	25 00
1669	Manzanillo	"	50 00	25 00
1836	Acapulco	"	60 00	30 00
2053	Port Angel	"	65 00	32 50
2138	Salina Cruz	"	65 00	32 50
2219	Tonala	"	65 00	32 50
2330	San Benito	"	65 00	32 50
2348	Ocos	Guatemala	75 00	37 50
2369	Champerico	"	75 00	37 50
2443	San Jose de Guatemala	"	75 00	37 50
2505	Acajutla	Salvador	75 00	37 50
2541	La Libertad	"	75 00	37 50
	El Triunfo	"	75 00	37 50
2653	La Union	"	75 00	37 50
2674	Amapala	Honduras	75 00	37 50
2741	Corinto	Nicaragua	80 00	40 00
2849	San Juan del Sur	"	80 00	40 00
3013	Punta Arenas	Costa Rica	80 00	40 00
3473	Panama	Colombia	100 00	50 00
4283	Guayaquil	Ecuador	155 00	65 00
4503	Payta	Peru	165 00	67 00
4664	Eten	"	167 00	70 00
4698	Pacasmayo	"	172 00	72 00
4764	Salaverry	"	175 00	72 00
5044	Callao	"	187 00	75 00
5516	Mollendo	"	195 00	77 00
5650	Arica	Chile	205 00	80 00
5721	Pisagua	"	205 00	80 00
5760	Iquique	"	205 00	82 00
5987	Antofagasta	"	210 00	85 00
6408	Coquimbo	"	220 00	90 00
6606	Valparaiso	"	225 00	90 00

Rates to East Coast of South America and Europe furnished on application. The holders of through tickets between San Francisco and Valparaiso can break their journey at any of the ports of call of steamers of either line, provided that the time between starting point and destination does not exceed three (3) months. Return tickets will be subject to 20 per cent. rebate.

Each passenger (adult) in first-class is allowed 20 cubic feet of space for baggage.

    RATING—Servants in Cabin, ⅔ fare.
       Children, 8 to 12 years, ½ fare.
         " 3 to 8 " ¼ "
         " Under 3 " 1 free.

CABIN AND DECK RATES

quoted herein from San Francisco to Mexican, Central American, Panama and South American Ports are temporarily reduced as follows:—

SAN FRANCISCO TO		CABIN	DECK
Mazatlan	Mexico	$ 22 50	$ 11 25
San Blas	"	25 00	12 50
Manzanillo	"	25 00	12 50
Acapulco	"	30 00	15 00
Port Angel ⎫	"	40 00	20 00
Salina Cruz ⎬ via Acapulco	"	45 00	22 50
Tonala ⎥	"	50 00	25 00
San Benito ⎭	"	55 00	27 50
Ocos	Guatemala	37 50	18 75
Champerico	"	37 50	18 75
San Jose de Guatemala	"	37 50	18 75
Acajutla	Salvador	37 50	18 75
La Libertad	"	37 50	18 75
El Triunfo	"	37 50	18 75
La Union	"	37 50	18 75
Amapala	Honduras	37 50	18 75
Corinto	Nicaragua	40 00	20 00
San Juan del Sur	"	40 00	20 00
Punta Arenas	Costa Rica	40 00	20 00
Panama	Colombia	50 00	25 00
Guayaquil	Ecuador	117 00	43 00
Payta	Peru	135 00	49 00
Eten	"	138 00	50 00
Pacasmayo	"	138 00	50 00
Salaverry	"	141 00	50 00
Callao	"	147 00	52 00
Mollendo	"	172 00	60 00
Arica	Chile	177 00	61 00
Pisagua	"	179 00	62 00
Iquique	"	179 00	62 00
Antofagasta	"	188 00	67 00
Coquimbo	"	199 00	70 00
Valparaiso	"	205 00	71 00

CABIN AND DECK RATES

quoted herein from San Francisco to Mexican, Central American, Panama and South American Ports are temporarily reduced as follows:—

SAN FRANCISCO TO		CABIN	DECK
Mazatlan	Mexico	$ 22 50	$ 11 25
San Blas	"	25 00	12 50
Manzanillo	"	25 00	12 50
Acapulco	"	30 00	15 00
Port Angel	"	40 00	20 00
Salina Cruz } via Acapulco	"	45 00	22 50
Tonala	"	50 00	25 00
San Benito	"	55 00	27 50
Ocos	Guatemala	37 50	18 75
Champerico	"	37 50	18 75
San Jose de Guatemala	"	37 50	18 75
Acajutla	Salvador	37 50	18 75
La Libertad	"	37 50	18 75
El Triunfo	"	37 50	18 75
La Union	"	37 50	18 75
Amapala	Honduras	37 50	18 75
Corinto	Nicaragua	40 00	20 00
San Juan del Sur	"	40 00	20 00
Punta Arenas	Costa Rica	40 00	20 00
Panama	Colombia	50 00	25 00
Guayaquil	Ecuador	117 00	43 00
Payta	Peru	135 00	49 00
Eten	"	138 00	50 00
Pacasmayo	"	138 00	50 00
Salaverry	"	141 00	50 00
Callao	"	147 00	52 00
Mollendo	"	172 00	60 00
Arica	Chile	177 00	61 00
Pisagua	"	179 00	62 00
Iquique	"	179 00	62 00
Antofagasta	"	188 00	67 00
Coquimbo	"	199 00	70 00
Valparaiso	"	205 00	71 00

The Pacific Steam Navigation Co.'s Fleet.

West Coast Lines of Steamers

		Tons			Tons
SANTIAGO		2953	PUNO		2398
SERENA		2394	PIZARRO		2160
MENDOZA		2160	ARICA		1771
ECUADOR		1768	QUITO		1089
MANAVI		1041	TALCA (Twin Screw)		1018
TABOGA		649	CHIRIQUI		643

Straits Line of Fast Mail Steamers

OROTAVA		5857	ORAVIA (Twin Screw)		5321
ORISSA (Twin Screw)		5317	OROPESA (Twin Screw)		5303
ORELLANA		4821	ORCANA		4803
IBERIA		4689	LIGURIA		4677

Straits Line of Cargo Boats

GALICIA (Twin Screw) Building	4750	SORATA		4581
CORCOVADO		4568	SARMIENTO	3603
INCA		3593	MAGELLAN	3590
ANTISANA		3584		

Steamers Running in the Orient Line

ORTONA (Twin Screw)		8000	ORIZABA		6298
OROYA		6297	ORUBA		5857

S. F. - Valparaiso Service

CALIFORNIA (Twin Screw) Bldg	6000	MEXICO (Twin Screw) Bldg.	6000
VICTORIA (Twin Screw) Bldg	6000	PANAMA (Twin Screw) Bldg.	6000
COLOMBIA (Twin Screw)	3500	GUATEMALA (Twin Screw)	3500
CHILE (Twin Screw)	3225	PERU (Twin Screw)	3225
AREQUIPA	2953		

Compañia Sud-Americana de Vapores' Fleet.

TUCAPEL	3061	
ACONCAGUA	2761	
LIMARI	2647	S. F. - Valparaiso Service
PALENA	2640	
LOA	2506	

IMPERIAL	2704	MAIPO	2621
CACHAPOAL	2308	LAUTARO	2085
MAPOCHA	2053	AMAZONAS	2009
ITATA	1971	MAULE	900
MALLECO	641	CHILLAN	624
LUMACO	636	CAUTIN	527
LIRCAI	517	PUDETO	298

COCHRAN & CO.
BIRKENHEAD, ENGLAND.

COCHRAN'S PATENT MULTITUBULAR BOILERS.

ACCESSIBLE FOR CLEANING.

ECONOMICAL IN FUEL.

ALL SIZES IN STOCK OR PROGRESS.

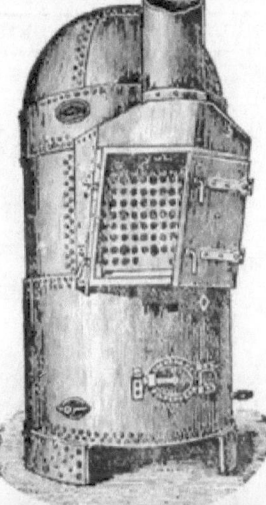

PRICE LISTS ON APPLICATION.

COMPOUND SURFACE CONDENSING, AND TRIPLE EXPANSION ENGINES.

IN STOCK OR PROGRESS.

PRICE LISTS ON APPLICATION.

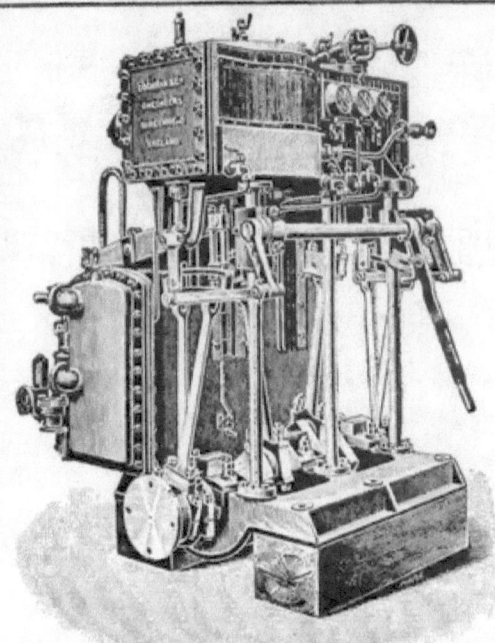

Telegraphic Address:—"MULTITUBE, BIRKENHEAD."   A.B.C. Code used

COCHRAN & CO
BIRKENHEAD, ENGLAND.

Telegraphic Address:—"MULTITUBE, BIRKENHEAD."   A.B.C. Code used.

SMALL RIVER STEAMERS.

STEAM LAUNCHES, YACHTS, TUGS, CARGO STEAMERS, BARGES, STERNWHEEL STEAMERS.

IN STOCK OR PROGRESS.

PRICE LISTS ON APPLICATION.

Facsimile of Label & Capsule.

Ayala Champagne

This Wine can also be had Extra Dry.

To be obtained on board the P. S. N. Co.'s Vessels.

FAC-SIMILE OF NECK BAND

Agents—W. & J. LOCKETT, Liverpool.

J. & F. MARTELL
COGNAC

V.O.
V.S.O.
V.S.O.P.
V.V.S.O.P.

Liverpool Agents—W. & J. LOCKETT.

GEORGE MACLELLAN & CO.

India Rubber, Asbestos and Waterproof Goods Manufacturers,

GLASGOW RUBBER WORKS,
MARYHILL, GLASGOW;
Warehouse—253 Argyle Street.

CONTRACTORS to the ADMIRALTY and WAR OFFICES.

India Rubber and Asbestos Goods of all kinds for Mechanical, Chemical, Electrical, and other purposes, as supplied to the British and Foreign Governments and the principal Shipping, Railway, Engineering and Ship-building Companies.

SPECIALITIES:

Patent Semi-Metallic Packings for Triple and Quadruple Expansion Engines, Valves, Beltings, Hose Pipes for Steam and Hydraulic Pressure Sheets for Tropical Climates, &c.

WATERPROOF GOODS.—Ladies' and Gentlemen's Garments, Rugs, Hold-alls, Fishing and Sporting Articles, Cart and Wagon Covers, Airproof Goods, Beds, Pillows, Cushions, &c.

BRANCHES:

LIVERPOOL—The Atlantic, 8 Brunswick Street.
LONDON—113 Fenchurch Street.
MANCHESTER—35 Market Street.
NEWCASTLE-ON-TYNE—5 Mosley Street.
SUNDERLAND—Borough Road.
CARDIFF—21 West Bute Street.
BELFAST—3 Albert Square.

W. H. ALLEN, SON & CO.

QUEEN'S ENGINEERING WORKS,
BEDFORD,
AND
19 GREAT GEORGE STREET, WESTMINSTER, S.W.

Formerly of York Street Works, Lambeth, London.

CENTRIFUGAL PUMPING ENGINES, FANS and ENGINES.

REVERSING ENGINES. All AUXILIARY ENGINES for MARINE WORK.

MANUFACTURERS OF
HIGH-SPEED ENGINES,
TRIPLE AND COMPOUND
Direct-Acting ENGINES & DYNAMOS for Electric Lighting,
COMPLETE INSTALLATIONS CARRIED OUT.

All the New Steamers of the PACIFIC STEAM NAVIGATION CO. have been Installed by us.

WILSON, SONS & CO.

LIMITED.

Steamship Agents and Proprietors of

COAL DEPÔTS

AT

ST. VINCENT, C.V.	RIO DE JANEIRO.	MONTE VIDEO.
PERNAMBUCO.	SANTOS.	LA PLATA.
BAHIA.	SAO PAULO.	BUENOS AYRES.

Also Branch Establishments at **CARDIFF** and **BARRY**.

Stocks of only the very best Descriptions of South Wales Steam Coal.

TUG BOATS AT ALL THE PORTS.

Workshops at **St. Vincent, Pernambuco, Bahia** and **Rio Janeiro**, with efficient modern Plant, where repairs of all descriptions are undertaken.

WILSON, SONS & CO. Limited, are the Sole Proprietors of the above Depôts and Branches, and any inquiries as regards prices, &c., should be addressed to the HEAD OFFICE:—

7 DRAPERS' GARDENS, LONDON, E.C.

Telegraphic Address at each place—"ANGLICUS."

The Beldam Packing and Rubber Co.

77 GRACECHURCH STREET, LONDON, E.C.

BELDAM'S WELL-KNOWN SPECIALITIES,

More extensively used than any others.

Metallic Packings, Corrugated Valves, Spring Neck Bush, Metallic Tube Stopper.

CAMBRIDGE ANTI-CLINKERING FURNACE BAR,

Great Saving by using Cambridge Bars.   No Alterations to Furnace Fittings.

Weavers and Manufacturers of Asbestos Goods of every description. Packings, Jointings, Cloth, Tape, &c. Contractors to The Admiralty, Russian, Italian, Spanish, Egyptian, Chilian, Brazilian, and Japanese Governments.

Circulars and Price Lists on application to

LONDON: 77 GRACECHURCH STREET.
LIVERPOOL: 112 The Albany, OLD HALL STREET.
GLASGOW: 109 HOPE STREET.
MANCHESTER: 9 CORPORATION STREET.

Telegrams—"CORRUGATED, LONDON."   "CENTRIFUGAL, LIVERPOOL."

KEILLER'S
PURE SOLUBLE COCOA
INVIGORATING & REFRESHING.

MANUFACTURED BY

James Keiller & Son, Ltd., Dundee and London.

Makers of the CELEBRATED DUNDEE MARMALADE, also JAMS, TABLE JELLIES, PEELS, BOTTLED FRUITS, CHOCOLATES, and every description of Confectionery.

SHIPPERS TO ALL PARTS OF THE WORLD.

W. ROSENBERG & CO.

46, 48 & 50 LIME STREET,

ALSO

ART GALLERY, 69 LIME STREET,

LIVERPOOL, ENGLAND,

Fine Art Publishers,

Picture Frame Manufacturers,

Manufacturers and Importers of all kinds of MOULDINGS
for Framing and Decorative purposes.

GOLDEN HOURS. AFTER M. GOODMAN

Every modern subject published in Engraving, Etching, and Photogravure, in Stock or on Exhibition at our Galleries.

For Oil Paintings, Water Colours, &c., we are in direct touch with all the eminent British Artists, and all our purchases are made direct from them.
Commissions of any kind promptly executed.
Manufacturers of modern fancily-framed bevelled Mirrors, in Oxydised Silver and all the newest designs.
Special Factory for the Manufacture of Show-card Frames.

Cuadros al oleo y aquarelas pintados por artistas eminentes.
Grabados, y foto-grabados.
Espejos de fantasia con lunas sesgadas y planas.
Molduras de todas clases para marcos y decoraciones.
Marcos de fantasia para retratos fotograficos.

W. ROSENBERG & CO.
46, 48 & 50 LIME STREET,
LIVERPOOL, ENGLAND.

(ESTABLISHED 1810.)

HARRISON'S
HIGH-CLASS ENGINE OIL,
MACHINERY OIL
CYLINDER OIL,
LARD OIL,
AND
COLLIERY LAMP OIL,

AS SUPPLIED TO

THE PACIFIC STEAM NAVIGATION COMPANY.
THE CUNARD STEAM-SHIP COMPANY, LTD.
THE WEST INDIA AND PACIFIC STEAM-SHIP CO., LTD.
THE LONDON AND NORTH-WESTERN RAILWAY.
AND MANY OTHERS.

Great Efficiency and Economy obtained by the use of the above Oils.

Prices, Samples, &c., from the Manufacturers,

ELIJAH HARRISON & CO.
65 SOUTH JOHN STREET,
LIVERPOOL.

Over Half-a-Century's Reputation
for Quality.

ROB^{T.} ROBERTS & CO.'S

CELEBRATED Tea AND Coffee.

TRADE MARK.

30, Bold Street, **LIVERPOOL.**

27, Mincing Lane, **LONDON,** E.C.

EST^D 1840.

SPECIAL QUOTATIONS IN BOND FOR SHIPPING ORDERS

Robt. Roberts & Co., Ltd.

The HARRIS FEED WATER FILTER.

Telegrams:
"WINDTIGHT," London

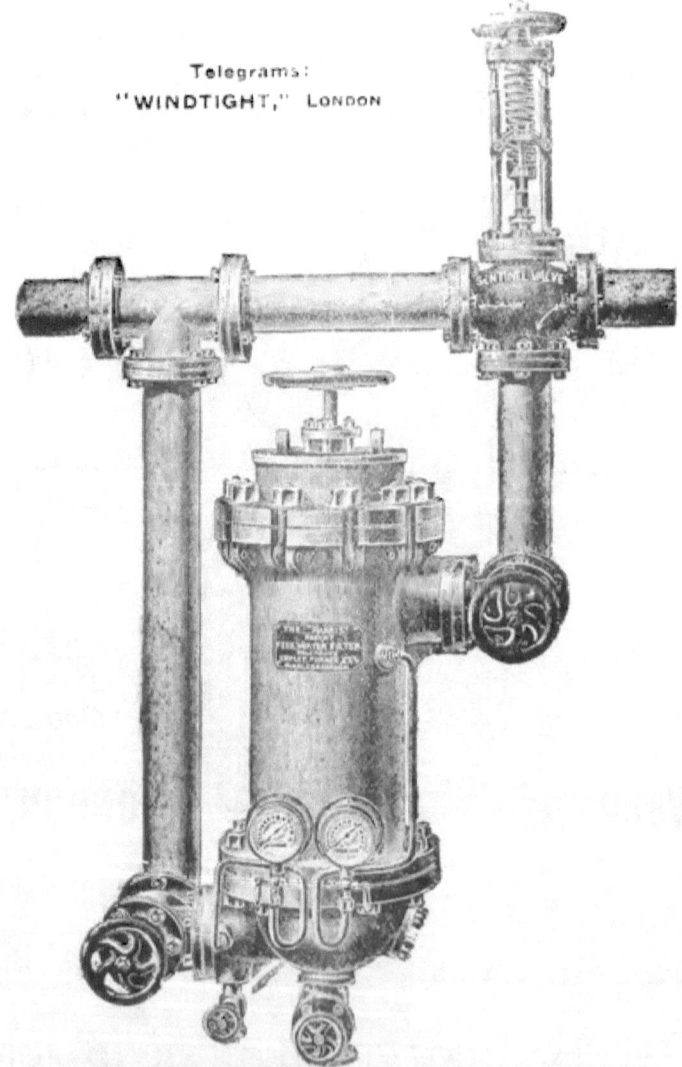

ANTHONY HARRIS, 73 Queen Victoria-St., London, E.C.

XVI.

THE

HARRIS FEED WATER FILTER

Is fitted to fifteen Steamers of the **Orient** and **Pacific Steam Navigation Companies**, to the principal Steamers of the **British Navy**, used solely in the **Cunard Company**, including the "**Campania**" and "**Lucania**;" also fitted in the **North German Lloyds, Russian Volunteer Fleet, Russian Navy, French Navy, Donald Currie Line, Rennie Line,** &c. &c. Fitted also to many of the largest Waterworks Plants, Electric Lighting Installations, and wherever Condensing Engines are used.

The Filtration of Feed Water for Boilers.

From the "MARINE ENGINEER."

"The efficient filtration of the feed water used in the boilers to generate steam in large ocean steamers driven at their top speed, has increasingly demanded the attention of engineers of late years, as the danger to the boilers and loss of fuel from the use of impure water has increased with the increase of pressure at which modern boilers are now worked. The most subtle and refractory impurity to be overcome is from the grease used in lubricating the pistons and valves and stuffing boxes of the engines, which after it has done its work is carried off with the steam into the condenser and returned with the feed water to the boiler, where it is brought into contact with the heating surfaces. In the "Campania" and "Lucania" the amount of water evaporated per day in raising steam amounts to over five thousand tons, and as the whole contents of the boilers is converted into steam and passes through the cylinders and condensers five times per day, carrying the grease along with it, it will be seen what an accumulation there would be by the end of the voyage were it not eliminated from the feed water as it passes back to the boilers. The Cunard Company in determining the class of feed filter to adopt in their great new liners were influenced by the success of one of the Harris filters fitted to another of their steamers. Their selection has been justified by the fact that on opening out the boilers of the Campania each run she has made both at New York and Liverpool they have been found entirely free from grease and the oxide and the brown dirt usually found in new boilers was also absent—notwithstanding the extra amount of lubricant used on the trial trip and initial voyages. The filters are self-cleansing, and the impurity is ejected by the reversal of the valves, so that the voyage to New York is completed without opening out or mechanically cleansing, which is a great relief to the engineers. The success which has attended the Harris filter in the great Cunarders has inundated Mr. Harris with orders and inquiries from all parts of the world, for land as well as marine purposes."

For Prices and Particulars apply to

ANTHONY HARRIS,

73 QUEEN VICTORIA-ST., LONDON, E.C.

Contractors to the British Admiralty.   Established 1838.

N. Hingley & Sons, Limited,

(SUCCESSORS TO THE NEW BRITISH IRON CO., 1894.)

NETHERTON & OLD HILL STEEL, IRON, CHAIN, CABLE, ANCHOR AND ENGINEERING WORKS,

Dudley, Staffordshire, England

MANUFACTURERS OF

"LION" IRON AND CHAINS.

STUD LINK CABLES OF THE HIGHEST CLASS.

NETHERTON SPECIAL BEST BEST CHAINS FOR MINING & CRAINS.

ANCHORS OF EVERY DESCRIPION.

SOLE MAKERS OF

HINGLEY'S & HALL'S PATENT STOCKLESS ANCHORS.

London:

62 Gracechurch Street, E.C.

Liverpool: Glasgow:

5 Chapel Street.   12 Waterloo Street.

Telegrams:
"HINGLEY, DUDLEY," and "STOCKLESS, LONDON."

CONTENTS.

—:o:—

	PAGE.
INDEX TO CONTENTS ...	XIX.
INDEX TO ADVERTISEMENTS ...	XXIV.
PREFACE	2
List of Standard Works on South America...	5
CHAPTER I.—The Pacific Steam Navigation Company	9-26
Court of Directors...	25
Executive Staff	26
Establishments Abroad	26
Principal Agents and Correspondents	27-29
Ships' Watches and Bells ...	30

EAST COAST OF SOUTH AMERICA.

CHAPTER II.—Brazilian Ports...	31-48
CHAPTER III.—The River Plate, Monte Video, Uruguay, Argentine Republic, Paraguay	49-57

CHAPTER IV.—**Straits of Magellan**	58-74

WEST COAST OF SOUTH AMERICA.

CHAPTER V.—Colombia ...	75-85
CHAPTER VI.—Ecuador ...	86-92
CHAPTER VII.—Peru	93-117
CHAPTER VIII.—Chile	118-148

CHAPTER IX.—**South American Currencies**	149-151

Map of South America	...FACE PREFACE
Track Chart to South America and Australia... ...	14a
Track Chart showing Pacific Line West Coast Service...	26a
Coats of Arms and Flags ...	31a
Chart of Straits of Magellan	58a

INDEX TO CONTENTS.

	PAGE.		PAGE.
Achataihua ...	110	Bolivia... ...	111–116
Aconcagua ...	142	Botafogo	41
Adrogué	54	Brillador ...	134
Alansi ...	90	Buenaventura	82
Albemarle ...	92	Buenos Ayres	52
Almendral ...	96	Buga	83
Ambato	90	Cachavi ...	86
Ancon ...	103	Cachinal ...	129
Ancud ...	148	Cachipascana	117
Andacollo	135	Cajamarca ...	97
Antisani	91	Calama ...	128
Antofagasta...	126	Calasnique ...	97
Apucuncarani	117	Calbuco	148
Aralar ...	127	Caldera ...	130
Arequipa	111	Caleta Buena	124
Arica ...	118	Cali	82
Ascope... ...	99	Galindo ...	99
Ascotan (Lake) ...	127–128	Callao	101
Asuncion ...	56	Campo Grande ...	36
Atacama	126–130	Cancana ...	120
Ayacucho	100	Cañete... ...	108
Bahia	35	Cape Boqueron ...	58
Bahia Blanca	55	Cape Espiritu Santo ...	58
Bahia (Ecuador)	86	Cape Froward ...	64
Balao ...	91	Cape Negro	60
Ballenita	88	Cape Pillar ...	70
Barbacoas ...	84	Cape St. Anthony	49
Barra do Pirahy ...	48	Cape St. Mary ...	49
Barranco	103	Cape St. Vincent	59
Bayos ...	127	Cape Virgins	58
Belgrano ...	54	Carabaya ...	115
Bio Bio (River) ...	146	Caracas River	86
Boa Vista ...	31	Caracoles	127
Bodegas	90–91	Carampangue Mines ...	146
Bogotá... ...	83	Carcot (Lake)	127

	PAGE.		PAGE.
Carioca Mountains	43	Chocope	99
Carrizal Alto	131	Chorrillos Bay	102
Carrizal Bajo	131	Chorrillos	103
Cartávio	99	Chosica	106
Casa Grande	99	Cobija	126
Casapalca	105	Cochabamba	114
Casma	100	Colico	146
Castrovireyna	109	Colon	82
Catacaos	94	Colquechaca	127
Cattete	41	Comendador Creek	93
Cauquenes Springs	142	Concepcion	107-144
Cazanga	32	Conchi	128
Cayalti	96	Conchicul	127
Cayambi	91	Constitucion	142-143
Cerro Azul	108	Copiapo	131
Cerro Blanco	132	Coquimbo	133
Cerro de Hoja	87	Coracora	110
Cerro de l'asco	106-107	Corcovado Mountain	43
Cerros de la Cruz	88	Cordova	56
Chafan	97	Cordoba	82
Chala	110	Coronel	144
Chan Chan	98	Coropuna	117
Chañaral	129	Corral	147
Chañarcillo	130	Cosquin	56
Chanchamayo	107	Cotopaxi	90
Charchani	117	Crooked Reach	68
Chepen	97	Cuenca	91
Chicama	99	Cuevitas	128
Chicla	106	Curanilahue	146
Chiclayo	95-96	Cuzco	114-116
Chililaya (Bolivia)	112	Cyapas	86
Chillan	144	Daule	91
Chimbo	90	Dawson Islands	59
Chimborazo	90	Desterro	47
Chimboté	99	Duran	90
Chimu	98	Elizabeth Island	60
Chincha	108	Esmeraldas	86
Chincha Islands	110	Eten	95
Chipicani	120		
Chiquitoy	99	Facalá	98

3

	PAGE.		PAGE.
Ferreñafe	96	Junin	125
Flamenco Island	81	Kenuta	120
Flores	54	La Paz	112-120
Fray Bentos	51	La Paz (Bolivia)	111
Freirina	132	La Punta	101
Galápagos Islands	92	Lambayeque	96
Galindo	99	Larangeiras	41
Gap Peak	58	Laraquete	146
Garanhuns	33	Laredo	99
Gavea	41-43	Las Animas	130
Glacier Bay	69	Latacunga	90
Guadalupe	97	Leba	146
Gualatieri	120	Lima	102
Guanaco	120	Limache	141
Guaranda	90	Llanquihue (Lake)	148
Guayacan	134	Loa	127
Guayaquil	88	Lobos de Afuera Islands	95
Guayas River	80	Lomas	110-127
Huacho	100	Lota	146
Huancavelica	109	Maceio	34
Huancayo	107	Machala	91
Huanchaca	128	Magdalena	103
Huanchaco	99	Mai Island	38
Huanuco	107	Mairo	107
Huarmey	100	Manaos	34
Huasco	132	Manta	87
Huaylas	100	Mar del Plata	55
Ica	109	Matucana	106
Ilha Raza	38	Mendoza	56
Illimani	117	Milagro	90
Ilo	117	Miraflores	103
Inca	127	Misti	111
Iquique	121	Mocollope	98
Itaparica Island	37	Mollendo	110
Jarillas	132	Monte Grande	97
Jauja	106	Monte Video	50
Jipijapa	87	Montecristi	87
Julaca	128	Moquegua	117
Juliaca	114	Mount Ancon	81

	PAGE		PAGE
Mount Buckland	63	Pilar	34
Mount Hermoso	100	Pimentel	95
Mount San Felipe	60	Pisagua	120
Mount Sarmiento	62	Pisco	109
Mount Tarn	60	Piura	94
Naranjal	91	Point las Piedras	49
Naranjito	90	Pomalca	96
Nazareth	34	Pomarape	120
Nitrate Oficinas	124	Port Famine	62
Nova Friburgo	45	Port Montt	148
		Porto Alegre	47
Olinda	32	Porto Bello	79
Olivo	134	Portoviejo	87
Oliagua	127-128	Potosi	113, 127
Ollanta	115	Pozuzo	107
Organ Mountains	45	Pucalá	96
Oroya	104	Puente	100
Oruro	113-120, 128	Puná (Island)	91
Ovalle	134-135	Puno	112
		Puquios	130
Pao d'Alho	34		
Pacasmayo	96	Quillota	141
Pai Island	38	Quito	90
Palmira	83		
Panama	79	Recife	31
Panuleillo	134	Rimac River	102
Paqueta	45	Rinconada	100
Paraguay	56	Riobamba	90
Parahyba	34	Rio Grande	47
Paranaguá	47	Rio de Janeiro	37
Parinacoto	120	Rio Minas Geraes	41
Pasto	85	Rio Vermelho	36
Patagonia	71-74	River Plate	49
Pátapo	95-96	Rosario	55
Paysandú	52	Sahama	120
Payta	93	Salado	130
Pelotas	47	Salaverry	98
Penco	144	Salinas	128
Pernambuco	31	Salto	52
Petropolis	44	Samanco	100
Pettagua	120	San Antonio	31-130
Philip Bay	59	San Bernardino	57
Pichincha	91	Sancholagua	91
Pichupichu	117	San Cristobal	127

XXIII.

	PAGE		PAGE
Sandy Point	60	Tanque	98
San Felipe	142	Tarma	106-107
San Isidro	62	Taulaté	48
San José	97	Tecape	97
San Pablo	127	Tembladera	97
San Pedro	97-127	Temperley	54
San Pedro de Lloc	97	Thiales	85
Santa Ana	87	Tierra del Fuego	65-67
Santa Barbara	109	Tijuca	44
Santa Elena	88	Timbauba	34
Santa Lucia	140	Tinogasta	131
Santa Rosa	91	Titicaca (Lake)	112
Santa Rosa (Cuzco)	111	Toco	125
Santa Thereza	46	Tocopilla	125
Sante Fé	55	Tolon	97
Santiago	139	Tomé	143
Santiago (Ecuador)	86	Tongoy	134
São Paulo	41-48	Trujillo	98
Saracoha (Lake)	117	Tucuman	55
Sousal	99	Tumaco	84
Saxihuaman	115	Tuman	96
Serena	133	Tumbes	93
Sibambe	90	Tunguragua	90
Sicuani	114	Tuquerros	85
Sorata	117	Ucayali River	107
Straits of Magellan	58	Una	33
S. Gorda	128	Urbinas	117
S. Salvador	35	Urubamba	115
Suchiman	100	Uruguay	51
Sucre	112	Uyuni	128
Supe	100	Valdivia	147
Sylvestre	46	Vallenar	133
Tacna	119	Valparaiso	136
Tacora	120	Victoria	30
Talambo	97	Vicuña	135
Talara	94	Vilcanota	117
Talca	142	Vina del Mar	141
Talcahuano	143	Vinzos	100
Taltal	129		
Tambo	115	Yaguachi	90
Tambo de Mora	108	Yonan	97
Tandli	55	Zorritos	93

INDEX TO ADVERTISEMENTS.

BANKS.

		PAGE
Bank of Liverpool, Ltd. ... Liverpool		165
London & Brazilian Bank, Ld. London		166
London & River Plate Bank, Limited ... ... London		166

DRUGS.

British Castor Co. Ld. ...	London	... Castor Oil	193
Johnson, J. H. & S. ...	Liverpool ...	... Drysaltery, Disinfectants, &c.	177

ENGINEERS, MACHINISTS, BOATBUILDERS, &c.

Allen, W. H., Son & Co.	... Bedford ...	... Engines, &c. ...	IX.
Cochran & Co.	... Birkenhead ...	... Boilers	II.
Cochran & Co.	... Birkenhead ...	... Steamers, Launches, Yachts, &c.	III.
Clarke, Chapman & Co.	... Gateshead-on-Tyne	Machinery, Engines, &c.	170
Edison & Swan United Electric Light Co. Ld. ...	London	... Electric Light Fittings, &c.	I.
Goodfellow, Benj.	Hyde ...	... Refrigerating Machinery, &c.	182
Harland & Wolff, Limited ...	Belfast	... Shipbuilders, Engineers	167
Harris, Anthony ...	... London	... Feed Water Filters	XV.-XVI.
Haslam Foundry and Engineering Co. Ld. ...	Derby ...	... Refrigerating Machinery, &c.	185
Hingley, N. & Sons ...	... Dudley	... Anchors and Chains	XVII.
Liverpool Engineering and Condenser Company ...	Liverpool	... Condensers, Filters, &c.	179
Lloyd & Lloyd	... Liverpool	... Tubes	198
Weir, G. & J. Ld. ...	... Glasgow	... Pumps, Evaporators	181
Wilson, Henry, & Co.	... Liverpool	... Hardware	189

FINE ARTS.

Rosenberg, W. & Co. ...	Liverpool ...	... Fine Arts	XII.

FURNISHING, OUTFITTING, ELECTRO-PLATE, LINEN, NAUTICAL INSTRUMENTS, &c.

Brintons, Limited ...	... Kidderminster	... Carpets	168
British P.P. Paper Co. ...	London	... Toilet Paper ...	164
Broadwood J. & Sons ...	... London	... Pianos ...	192

XXV.

FURNISHING, &c.—continued.

			PAGE
Chadburn & Son	... Liverpool	... Telegraphs, &c.	188
Collard & Collard	... London	... Pianos	186
Cook & Townshend	... Liverpool	... Furniture, Bedding, &c.	191
Elkington & Co.	... Liverpool	... Electro-Plate	194
Ray, J. W. & Co.	... Liverpool	... Nautical Instruments	195
Richardson, Sons & Owden, Limited	... Belfast	... Linen	VII.
Walker & Hall	... Sheffield	... Electro-Plate	192

HOTELS.

		PAGE
Adelphi	... Liverpool	161
Grande Hotel Metropole	... Rio de Janeiro	164
Hotel Oriental	... Monte Video	162
Hotel Sul-Americano	... Bahia	165
Midland Grand	... London	166

INDIA RUBBER, ASBESTOS, &c.

			PAGE
Beldam Packing & Rubber Co.	London	... Valves, &c.	XI.
Maclellan, George & Co.	... Glasgow	... Valves, &c.	VIII.

LEATHER MERCHANTS.

			PAGE
Angus, George & Co.	... Newcastle-on-Tyne	, Belting, &c.	197

OILS, ENGINE &c.

		PAGE
Bremner, John A. & Co.	... London	180
Harrison, Elijah & Co.	... Liverpool	XIII.
Crane, P. Moir, & Co.	... Manchester	169
Oakbank Oil Co. Ld.	... Glasgow	171

PRINTING AND STATIONERY.

			PAGE
Rockliff Bros. Ltd.	... Liverpool	... Printing and Stationery	187

RAILWAYS.

		PAGE
Central Argentine	... Buenos Ayres	156
Buenos Ayres and Rosario	... Buenos Ayres	157

SHIP STORE DEALERS, PAINTS, ROPES, CANVAS, &c.

			PAGE
Anglo-Swiss Condensed Milk Company	... London	... Milk	190
Bell Brothers & Thomson	... Liverpool	... Ship's Stores	183
Jackson, McConnan and Temple	... Liverpool	... Ropes, Cordage, Oakum, &c.	172
Hampson, B. H.	... Stockport	... Waste, Sponge Cloths	175

SHIP STORE DEALERS, &c.—continued.

			PAGE
Keiller, James, & Son	Dundee	Marmalade, Jams, &c.	XI.
Mackenzie & Mackenzie	Edinburgh	Biscuits	176
Minton, R. R. & Co	Liverpool	Paints, Colors, Varnishes	168
Port Glasgow & Newark Sail Cloth Co.	Port Glasgow	Sailcloth, Canvas	178
Roberts, Robert, & Co. Ltd.	Liverpool	Tea & Coffee	XIV.

SOAP.

Pears, A. & F. Ld.	London		201

STEAM-SHIP LINES, AGENTS, & MARINE INSURANCE COMPANIES.

Cook, Thomas, & Son	London	Tourist Agents	158
Orient Line	London		154
Pacific Line	Liverpool		152
Pacific Line (Pyrenees Tours)	Liverpool		153
Pacific Line—Tours round South America, and *via* New York	Liverpool		199
Thames & Mersey Marine Insurance Co.	Liverpool and London		159
White Star Line	Liverpool		155
Wilson, Sons & Co. Ld.	London		X.

WINES, SPIRITS, MINERAL WATERS.

Ayala & Co.	Chateau d'Ay	Champagne	V.
Apollinaris Co. Ld.	London	Apollinaris Water	200
Ihlers & Bell	Liverpool	Ale & Stout	196
Johannis, Ld.	London	Johannis Table Water	174
Lockett, W. & J.	Liverpool	Whiskey	IV.
Martell, J. & F.	Cognac	Brandy	VI.
Nicholson, J. & W. & Co.	London	Gin	187
Ross, W. A. & Sons, Ld.	Belfast	Aerated Table Waters	173
Schweppe, J. & Co.	London	Mineral Waters	184

Pacific Line

Guide to South America

Containing information for

TRAVELLERS AND SHIPPERS

TO PORTS ON THE

EAST AND WEST COASTS

OF SOUTH AMERICA

Price 2/6 net.

LONDON.
SIMPKIN, MARSHALL, HAMILTON, KENT & Co. Ltd. PUBLISHERS, 4, STATIONERS HALL COURT, E.C.

LIVERPOOL.
ROCKLIFF BROTHERS, Ltd., PRINTERS AND STATIONERS, 44, CASTLE STREET.

1895.

Entered at Stationers' Hall. *All Rights Reserved.*

F2223
.P2

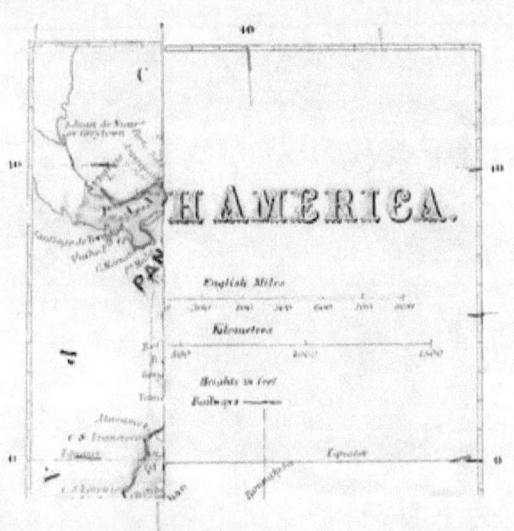

PREFACE.

THE information given in this Guide Book has been obtained from the most reliable sources, and has been specially compiled for the use of Travellers and Shippers by the Steamers of THE PACIFIC STEAM NAVIGATION CO. It will also be of value to anyone desirous of becoming acquainted with the Brazilian and River Plate Ports, the Straits of Magellan, and the West Coast of South America.

The particulars of times of departure of steamers and trains, and also hotel charges, are of course subject to variation, and, as a matter of precaution, travellers should verify same by inquiry from the Pacific Company's Agent at the port concerned. In cases also in which hotels are not referred to, the several Agents of the Company will readily furnish any information required.

This work is not intended to replace the Hand-books—published by The Pacific Company,

PREFACE.

THE information given in this Guide Book has been obtained from the most reliable sources, and has been specially compiled for the use of Travellers and Shippers by the Steamers of THE PACIFIC STEAM NAVIGATION Co. It will also be of value to anyone desirous of becoming acquainted with the Brazilian and River Plate Ports, the Straits of Magellan, and the West Coast of South America.

The particulars of times of departure of steamers and trains, and also hotel charges, are of course subject to variation, and, as a matter of precaution, travellers should verify same by inquiry from the Pacific Company's Agent at the port concerned. In cases also in which hotels are not referred to, the several Agents of the Company will readily furnish any information required.

This work is not intended to replace the Hand-books—published by The Pacific Company, and issued gratis—giving precise details of their Service from Europe to South America, and of their several Services on the West Coast of the last-named Continent; but has been written to meet a want which has frequently been felt and expressed.

It will be seen, from the contents, that a voyage to the East and West Coasts of South America, whether it be performed by the Naturalist or Botanist, in the gratification of that wish to visit the tropics which every scientist must feel; by the traveller in pursuit of recreation, or by the invalid in search of health, will afford the means of amply satisfying each special need. The scientist will find vast fields for the carrying on of his favourite study; the traveller varied and beautiful scenes in the Straits of Magellan and objects of interest in every port of call; and the invalid, especially if he be suffering from any pulmonary disease, will find in Bolivia particularly, and in other parts of the South American Republics, that dry and rarified atmosphere so essential to complete restoration.

The Company's Agents have rendered valuable assistance in the compilation of this Book, and reference has also been made to the undermentioned Standard Works, which travellers to those of the South American Republics specially dealt with would do well to peruse:—

Brazil—

"A Year in Brazil."
H. DENT, 1886.

"3000 Miles through Brazil."
J. W. WELLS, 1886.

"Eleven Weeks in North-Eastern Brazil."
W. A. FORBES, 1885.

"Hand-book of Rio," issued by the Editor of "Rio News."

Uruguay.—

"Its Geography, History, Rural Industries and Commerce."   Official Publication, 1883.

Argentina.—

"Cameos from the Silver Land."
E. W. WHITE, 1881.

"The River Plate as a Field for Emigration."
LATZINA, 1883.

"Eight Months in the Granchaco of the Argentine Republic."   G. PELLESCHI, 1886.

"The Naturalist in La Plata."
W. H. HUDSON, 1892.

"Argentina and the Argentines."
T. A. TURNER, 1892.

Paraguay.—

"Paraguay in 1893."

G. LENNOX.

Patagonia

"At Home with the Patagonians."

G. C. MUSTER, 1871.

"Across Patagonia."

LADY FLORENCE DIXIE.

"Cruise of the Alert."

R. W. COPPINGER, 1883.

"Idle Days in Patagonia."

W. H. HUDSON, 1893.

"Journal of Researches into the Natural History and Geology of the Countries visited during the Voyage round the World of H.M.S. 'Beagle.'"

CHARLES DARWIN, 1890.

Chili—

"Chili and the River Plate in 1891."

G. C. MORANT.

"The South American Pilot."

STAFF-COM. J. PENN, 1872.

It being felt that a short history of the pioneer and still leading Company to the Pacific would be of interest to the travelling public, and would form a suitable introduction to this work, the same has been made the subject of Chapter I.

R.M.S. "ORUBA," 5552 TONS.

CHAPTER I.

THE
Pacific Steam Navigation Company.

ON the 17*th* February, 1840, just about the time that transatlantic navigation was an assured success, a charter was obtained "under letters patent" for the establishment of this Company, with a small subsidy for the conveyance of the British Mails along the shores of the Pacific. The capital of the Company was at first limited to £250,000 in shares of £50 each, the whole of which was subscribed for, but only an amount was called up sufficient at the time to enable the Directors to provide two boats— the "Chile" and "Peru"—which were dispatched to commence operations towards the close of 1840. These vessels were wooden paddle wheel steamers, sister ships, of 700 tons register, with engines of about 150 horse-power; their extreme length being 198 feet, and extreme breadth 50 feet. They were at that time considered fine vessels, and on their arrival at Valparaiso they were received with great rejoicings and with salvos of artillery—everybody wishing to visit them; the President of the Chilian Republic, with his Ministers, being the first to welcome the steamships to the shores of the Pacific. From this small beginning was developed the vast trade that now exists between South America and Great Britain.

The Company in its early days had many difficulties to overcome, the scarcity of fuel being one of the greatest; and during the first five years the steamers were worked at a loss. Notwithstanding this, the shareholders resolved to persevere, and the fleet was gradually augmented.

In 1852 four new steamers, viz., the "Lima," "Santiago," "Quito," and "Bogota," of about 1100 tons and 450 horse-power each, were added to the line, to be employed in a bi-monthly service between Valparaiso and Panama. From that time the trade in the Pacific rapidly developed, new and hitherto unthought of branches of commerce were opened up, and the success of the Company was assured.

THE "LIMA," "SANTIAGO," "QUITO," AND "BOGOTA."

The Directors commenced to apply the compound engine to their steamships in 1856, thus effecting considerable economy in the matter of coal consumption; and it is worthy of record that the Company were not only the first to adopt compound engines for ocean-going steamers, but were almost singular in this respect for upwards of 14 years.

In 1865 the chartered powers of the Company were extended to the establishment of lines "between the West Coast of South America and the River Plate, including the Falkland Islands and such other ports or places in North and South America, and other foreign ports, as the said Company shall deem expedient."

In December, 1867, at a special meeting of the shareholders, it was determined to add to the operations of the Company a monthly line from Liverpool to the West Coast of South America, *via* the Straits of Magellan. This entirely new and important, though hazardous branch of the service, necessitated an increase of the capital of the Company to £2,000,000.

In May, 1868, the paddle-wheeler "Pacific," of 1630 tons and 450 horse-power, was despatched from **Valparaiso to Liverpool**, as the pioneer of the new mail line. The project was successful, and in 1870 it was determined to extend the voyages beyond Valparaiso, making the terminal port Callao, and to increase the number to three a month.

In January, 1872, the capital was increased to £3,000,000 in order to enable the Company to establish a weekly line from Liverpool to Callao—a distance of 11,000 miles—and on the 8*th* of January, 1873, the steamship "Sorata," 4038 tons, and 4000 horse-power, sailed from Liverpool as the first vessel under the new contract with Her Majesty's Government for a regular weekly service to and from Callao, with calls at Bordeaux, Spanish Ports, Lisbon, Rio de Janeiro, Monte Video, and Sandy Point in the Straits of Magellan.

To carry out and maintain this service efficiently, and in order to provide also for the increasing demands for additional tonnage on the West Coast of South America, it became necessary to considerably augment the fleet, and by 1874 the Company had no fewer than 54 steamers in commission, with an aggregate tonnage of 120,000, and of an aggregate horse-power (nominal) of 21,395. These were probably the finest and best appointed vessels in the mercantile marine of any nation.

The promises of a lucrative traffic were eventually, however, not fulfilled; the trade with South America fell off; and an extraordinary increase in the price of coal and other necessaries added so much to the cost of working the line that the weekly sailings had to be abandoned, and the fortnightly service, which is now in force, reverted to.

Employment had then to be found for the steamers

R.M.S. "OROYA," 6057 TONS.

Pacific Line Steamers.
Track Chart to South America & Australia.

which were not required for the West Coast business; and an opportunity was soon afforded by the establishment of the Orient Line from London to Australia, which was commenced with the steamship "Lusitania" early in 1877, and monthly sailings were maintained with five of the Company's steamers, until January, 1880, when, under an arrangement with the Orient Steam Navigation Company, the fortnightly line to Australia was established. Four of the finest vessels of the Company, viz., "Orizaba," "Oroya," "Oruba," and "Orotava," are now engaged in that trade. The Capital is now reduced to £1,477,125.

The fleet of the Company at present consists of the following screw steamships :—

	Tons Gross Reg.	H.P. Effec.		Tons Gross Reg.	H.P. Effec.
Orizaba	6077	7000	Araucania	2884	2000
Oroya	6057	7000	Puno	2398	2000
Orotava	5552	7000	Serena	2394	2000
Oruba	5552	7000	Pizarro	2160	2000
Oropesa (twin screw)	5317	5000	Mendoza	2160	2000
Orissa	5317	5000	Bolivia	1925	1500
Orellana	4821	4500	Ayacucho	1916	1500
Oreana	4803	4500	Coquimbo	1821	1500
Iberia	4661	4500	Arica	1771	1250
Liguria	4648	4500	Ecuador	1768	1250
Potosi	4230	4000	Quito	1089	1000
Galicia	3835	4000	Manavi	1041	1000
Sarmiento	3603	3000	Arauco	801	500
Inca	3593	3000	Chala	598	300
Magellan	3590	3000	Casma	592	300
Antisana	3584	3000	Osorno (twin screw)	532	300
Arequipa	2952	3000	Assistance	200	120
Santiago	2952	3000	Morro (twin screw)	170	100

which were not required for the West Coast business; and an opportunity was soon afforded by the establishment of the Orient Line from London to Australia, which was commenced with the steamship "Lusitania" early in 1877, and monthly sailings were maintained with five of the Company's steamers, until January, 1880, when, under an arrangement with the Orient Steam Navigation Company, the fortnightly line to Australia was established. Four of the finest vessels of the Company, viz., "Orizaba," "Oroya," "Oruba," and "Orotava," are now engaged in that trade. The Capital is now reduced to £1,477,125.

The fleet of the Company at present consists of the following screw steamships:—

	Tons Gross Reg.	H.P. Effec.		Tons Gross Reg.	H.P. Effec.
Orizaba	6077	7000	Araucania	2884	2000
Oroya	6057	7000	Puno	2398	2000
Orotava	5552	7000	Serena	2394	2000
Oruba	5552	7000	Pizarro	2160	2000
Oropesa (twin screw)	5317	5000	Mendoza	2160	2000
Orissa " "	5317	5000	Bolivia	1925	1500
Orellana	4821	4500	Ayacucho	1916	1500
Oreana	4803	4500	Coquimbo	1821	1500
Iberia	4661	4500	Arica	1771	1250
Liguria	4648	4500	Ecuador	1768	1250
Potosi	4230	4000	Quito	1089	1000
Galicia	3835	4000	Manavi	1041	1000
Sarmiento	3603	3000	Arauco	801	500
Inca	3593	3000	Chala	598	300
Magellan	3590	3000	Casma	592	300
Antisana	3584	3000	Osorno (twin screw)	532	300
Arequipa	2952	3000	Assistance	200	120
Santiago	2952	3000	Morro (twin screw)	170	100

We describe fully, further on, the twin screw steamer "Oropesa,"—which vessel and her sister ship the "Orissa" form the latest additions to the fleet,—as a fair specimen of the Company's steamers in the Pacific Line to Valparaiso, all of which are provided with spacious cabins and saloons, and are fitted throughout with every modern convenience and accommodation for large numbers of passengers. The "Oropesa" and "Orissa" have already made a good reputation for speed and comfort in the trade to the East and West Coasts of South America. The remaining ships of the fleet are employed in the Straits of Magellan Lines of Mail and Cargo Steamers, and on the West Coast of South America. The West Coast Line connects via Panama with the various Atlantic Lines to Europe, and steamers to Central America and New York.

We now proceed to describe the general construction and passenger accommodation of the "Oropesa." She was built by Messrs. Harland and Wolff, Limited, Belfast, in the same yard in which the "Orellana" and "Oreana" were built one year previously. Her measurements are :— length 420 feet between perpendiculars, beam 48 feet 6 inches, and depth 36 feet to spar-deck. Her net registered tonnage is 3318 tons and gross 5317. She has four laid decks, besides a spacious promenade and boat-deck, extending the full length of the amidship houses, which serves as a shade for the upper-deck. Her hull is built of steel of ample thickness, and she is divided

R.M.S. "OROTAVA," 5552 TONS.

into watertight compartments, adding materially to the safety of the ship. In addition to the ordinary keel, she has two twelve-inch bilge keels, which materially assist in steadying the vessel in a heavy sea-way, while evidently in nowise checking speed. She is built with a double bottom—an additional element of safety—and between the two there are water-ballast tanks capable of holding 850 tons of water. Her engines, which are on the "triple expansion" principle, are of a very powerful description, and were also built by Messrs. Harland and Wolff, Limited. The dimensions of the cylinders are $23\frac{1}{2}$, $38\frac{1}{2}$ and 64 inches, and the stroke 48 inches. Aspinall's patent governors are fitted to the engines. Steam is supplied to the engines by four steel boilers, two double and two single-ended, which work at a pressure of 180 lbs. to the square inch. A donkey boiler, 10 feet 3 inches by 8 feet 6 inches, supplies the necessary steam for working the ship in port. These boilers have been tested up to 360 lbs., and have altogether a heating surface of 12,300 square feet. The auxiliaries are Quiggin's (Liverpool) feed heaters, evaporator and fresh water condensers, Harris's feed-water filter, two of G. Weir's feed pumps and one auxiliary pump, Harland and Wolff's own patent centrifugal circulating pumps and duplex ballast pumping gear, Carruther's duplex donkey pump for fresh water service throughout the ship, surface condenser for all waste steam of winches, heating, &c. Two single dynamo engines are supplied by Messrs. W. H.

Allen, Son & Co., London, who have fitted the electric lighting plant, no fewer than 457 lamps being in use. The refrigerating plant is very complete, a 20,000 cubic feet machine having been provided by The Haslam Foundry and Engineering Co., Derby. This machine is for the use of the ship's provisions only. The deck, mooring, cargo, and other appliances are very substantial, and are fitted with special regard to the requirements of the trade. The windlass is one of Messrs. Clarke, Chapman & Co.'s, and the six deck winches are by Messrs. J. H. Wilson & Co., Liverpool, the side hatches peculiar to this fleet being perpetuated. A complete set of telegraphs has been furnished by Messrs. J. W. Ray & Co., Liverpool, and are fitted on the forecastle, in the crow's nest, and in the wheelhouse aft and into the engine-room, where that firm's patent direct engine tell-tale indicators are fitted. She is fitted with Lord Kelvin's patent compasses and sounding machine. The steam steering gear is Messrs. Wilson and Pirrie's; the leading features being the facility with which it can be disconnected and the hand gear coupled, and the compression of both springs when any undue strain is put upon the rudder.

The forward "between decks" is arranged for fitting portable berths, and the total number of steerage passengers that can be berthed is 582. The saloon is on the main deck,

and is provided with seating accommodation for 70 first-class passengers. The panelling and pilasters all round, which are of oak, are handsomely carved in heavy relief, while the side port embayment, and the furniture, are in walnut. The ceiling is very prettily panelled in white and gold, and the apartment, which extends across the ship, has a rich and substantial appearance. The drawing-room opens off the staircase, and is elaborately decorated. The upper portion is in artistically panelled and carved sycamore, relieved by richly-carved walnut pilasters, and the lower is in walnut. The ceiling of this room is very pretty. Writing tables and bookcases are to match, and the easy chairs, lounges, and side settees are suitably upholstered in flowered peacock blue cloth, and bordered with old gold plush. A rich velvet pile carpet, and very fine dome skylight, which also serves the saloon, completes as charming a room as the most fastidious passenger might desire. Abaft the drawing-room, but opening on the same (upper) deck, is a most delightful first-class smoke-room, laid out in a very novel and luxurious style. The panelling is of oak of the moulding pattern, and carved on top. The furniture and lower wainscoting are of walnut. At each side of the four corners of the room squares have been formed, which afford convenient "locales" for card parties, &c. Other tables are placed in different positions as required. The chairs and other seats, which are of walnut, are upholstered in dark-coloured leather. The floor is covered with Harland's patent rubber tiles. Abaft, on the same deck, are the surgery, officers' and doctor's rooms, office, &c., opening on to the deck. A house on the after part of the deck contains the second-class smoke-room and companion-way, steward's room, and wheelhouse. A boat platform deck runs out to the side, nearly the full length of the house. The first-class passengers' berths are situated on the main deck forward of the saloon, and accommodation is provided for 91 persons. The rooms are commodious and well fitted, all hooks and other fittings being silver-plated. A large pantry is placed amidship abaft the saloon, and can be communicated with by a sliding bevelled glass panel in the saloon. The saloon galley is situated abaft the pantry. Farther aft is a most excellent arrangement of bath rooms and lavatories, those for gentlemen being on the starboard side, and those for ladies on the port. Still further aft are the junior officers', engineers', and other rooms. The alleyways on either side of them connect with the second-class dining saloon, a very fine, comfortable, and commodious cabin, in which the decorations are carried out in white enamel, teak and mahogany, the furniture being of the latter wood. The second-class berths are in the alleyways abaft the dining-room; these are roomy and well finished. Bath-rooms, lavatories, &c., all excellently appointed, are placed abaft of the rooms, and are on the same principle as the first-class. Accommodation is provided for 94 second-class passengers.

The Pacific Company's steamers are "first favourites" with the travelling public. The cuisine, cleanliness, ventilation, and lighting are carefully looked after; and the ships are well manned in every department. The Company in their underwriting accounts practically take the risk on their steamers, and the greatest care is naturally exercised in the selection of all Officers.

The Court of Directors of The Pacific Steam Navigation Company is composed of the following gentlemen:—

ROBERT RANKIN, Esq., Chairman (Messrs. Rankin, Gilmour & Co., British and Foreign Steamship Company, Limited—" Saint " Line).

E. PERCY BATES, Esq., J.P., Deputy-Chairman (Messrs. Edward Bates & Sons, Steamship Owners, &c.)

ALEXANDER ELDER, Esq. Chairman, British and African Steam Navigation Company, Limited).

JAMES G. NICHOLSON, Esq. (Chairman, Standard Marine Insurance Company, Limited).

WILLIAM HENRY SHIRLEY, Esq. (late partner with
Messrs. James Moss & Co.—" Moss " Line).

WILLIAM THOMSON, Esq. (Messrs. W. & R.
Thomson, Bedouin Steam Navigation Company).

EXECUTIVE STAFF.

LIVERPOOL:—

Joint Manager and Secretary	FREDERICK ALCOCK.
Joint Manager	HENRY WARD.
Accountant ...	JAMES WALKER.
Marine Superintendent	G. N. CONLAN.
Supt. Engineer	JAMES THOMSON.

COMPANY'S ESTABLISHMENTS ABROAD.

LA PALLICE AND BORDEAUX:—

Agent	HENRY DAVIS.

WEST COAST OF SOUTH AMERICA:—

Manager & Supt. Engineer ...	GEORGE SHARPE, Callao.
Agent	JOHN PRAIN, Valparaiso.
Agent	FRED. T. BASS, Panama.

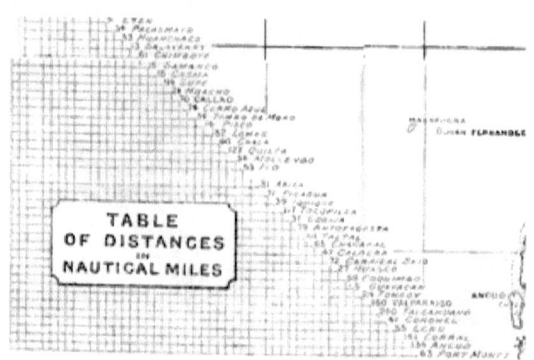

PRINCIPAL AGENTS AND CORRESPONDENTS.

EUROPE.

LONDON	ANDERSON, ANDERSON & Co., 5 Fenchurch Avenue, E.C. and 10 Cockspur Street, S.W.
Plymouth	J. PENGELLY & Co.
Manchester	A. W. WILSON, 67 Piccadilly.
Birmingham	REYNOLD ROGERS, 27 Cambridge Street.
Bradford	ROBERT JOHNSTON, 45 Brook Street.
Dundee	DAVID BRUCE & Co., 3 Royal Exchange Place.
Glasgow	J. DUNN & SONS, 107 St. Vincent Street.
Belfast	THOMSON & Co., 25 Victoria Street.
Hamburg	ERNST NIEBUHR, Jun.
Antwerp	AUG. SCHMITZ & Co.
Havre	THE CUNARD STEAMSHIP COMPANY, LIMITED.
PARIS	THE CUNARD STEAMSHIP COMPANY, LIMITED, 38 Avenue de l'Opera. LACRETTE & AMBROISE.
Genoa	VICTOR SAUVAIGUE. F. SCERNI.
Marseilles	F. PUTHET & Co.
Santander	DORIGA & HIJOS Y BOTIN.
Corunna	SOBRINOS DE JOSÉ PASTOR.
Carril and Vigo	BARCENA Y FRANCO.
MADRID	LESPES Y ESNAOLA.
LISBON	E. PINTO BASTO & Co.
Oporto	H. KENDALL & Co.
Madeira	BLANDY BROTHERS & Co.
Santa Cruz (Teneriffe)	HAMILTON & Co.
St. Vincent	WILSON, SONS & Co., LIMITED.

EAST COAST.

Pernambuco	WILSON, SONS & Co., LIMITED.
Bahia	WILSON, SONS & Co., LIMITED.
Rio Janeiro	WILSON, SONS & Co., LIMITED.
Monte Video	WILSON, SONS & Co., LIMITED.
Buenos Ayres	WILSON, SONS & Co., LIMITED.
Sandy Point	R. STUBENRAUCH.
Falkland Islands (Stanley)	A. E. BAILLON.
GENERALLY	THOMAS COOK & SON.

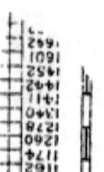

PRINCIPAL AGENTS AND CORRESPONDENTS.

EUROPE.
LONDON	ANDERSON, ANDERSON & Co., 5 Fenchurch Avenue, E.C. and 10 Cockspur Street, S.W.
Plymouth	J. PENGELLY & Co.
Manchester	A. W. WILSON, 67 Piccadilly.
Birmingham	REYNOLD ROGERS, 27 Cambridge Street.
Bradford	ROBERT JOHNSTON, 45 Brook Street.
Dundee	DAVID BRUCE & Co., 3 Royal Exchange Place.
Glasgow	J. DUNN & SONS, 107 St. Vincent Street.
Belfast	THOMSON & Co., 25 Victoria Street.
Hamburg	ERNST NIEBUHR, Jun.
Antwerp	AUG. SCHMITZ & Co.
Havre	THE CUNARD STEAMSHIP COMPANY, LIMITED.
PARIS	THE CUNARD STEAMSHIP COMPANY, LIMITED, 38 Avenue de l'Opera. LAURETTE & AMBROISE.
Genoa	VICTOR SAUVAIGUE. F. SCERNI.
Marseilles	F. PUTHET & Co.
Santander	DORIGA & HIJOS Y BOTIN.
Corunna	SOBRINOS DE JOSE PASTOR.
Carril and Vigo	BARCENA Y FRANCO.
MADRID	LESPES Y ESNAOLA.
LISBON	E. PINTO BASTO & Co.
Oporto	H. KENDALL & Co.
Madeira	BLANDY BROTHERS & Co.
Santa Cruz (Teneriffe)	HAMILTON & Co.
St. Vincent	WILSON, SONS & Co., LIMITED.

EAST COAST.
Pernambuco	WILSON, SONS & Co., LIMITED.
Bahia	WILSON, SONS & Co., LIMITED.
Rio Janeiro	WILSON, SONS & Co., LIMITED.
Monte Video	WILSON, SONS & Co., LIMITED.
Buenos Ayres	WILSON, SONS & Co., LIMITED.
Sandy Point	R. STUBENRAUCH.
Falkland Islands (Stanley)	A. E. BAILLON.
GENERALLY	THOMAS COOK & SON.

WEST COAST

Port	Agent
Punta Arenas (Costa Rica)	Rohrmoser & Co.
Pedregal	Lastra Hermanos
Sona	M. J. Grajales.
Agua Dulce	S. Sucre, J.
Buenaventura	R. G. de Paredes.
Tumaco	Gaminara & Leedee.
Esmeraldas	Servat & Dumarest.
Bahia (Ecuador)	Cia. de Agencias.
Manta	R. Delgado.
Cayo	San Lucas y Ca.
Ballenita	Pedro Infante.
Guayaquil	Geo. Chambers & Co.
Payta	F. P. Lopez & Co.
Pimentel	William V. Fry.
Eten	Supt. del Ferro-Carril.
Pacasmayo	Kauffmann & Co.
Malabrigo	Do.
Huanchaco	E. Gottfried é Hermanos.
Salaverry	Do.
Santa	Agustin Aste.
Chimbote	G. Valdeavellano.
Samanco	Guillermo Gaymer.
Casma	E. Farromeque é Hijos.
Huarmey	Servat Hermanos.
Supe	Thomas Valega.
Huacho	Pedro McGregor.
Chancay	F. Garmendia.
Cerro Azul	Henry Swayne.
Tambo de Mora	Luis Dagnino.
Pisco	J. J. Venn.
Lomas	Andres Casalino.
Chala	C. E. Bush.
Mollendo	James Golding.
Ilo	Gambetta Hermanos y Ca.
Arica	Viuda de Nugent y Ca.
Pisagua	Watters Brothers.
Junin	Richardson & Co.
Caleta Buena	Agua Santa Nitrate & Railway Co.

Iquique	North & Jewell.
Huanillos	Administrador del Cargüio de Huano.
Tocopilla	W. H. Williams.
Cobija	Artola Hermanos.
Antofogasta	Barnett & Co.
Paposo	Flavio Zuleta.
Taltal	Schjolberg & Co.
Chanaral	James G. Sheriff.
Caldera	H. P. Beazley.
Carrizal Bajo	Diaz & Co.
Huasco	Craig & Sons.
Pena Blanca	
Totoralillo	J. y P. P. Munoz.
Coquimbo } Guayacan }	
Tongoy	F. A. Bedwell.
Los Vilos	José M. del Rio.
Santiago	Swinburn & Co.
Tome	Henry A. Ward.
Penco	
Talcahuano } Concepcion }	Williamson, Balfour & Co.
Coronel	A. J. Franklin.
Lota	Lea & Co.
Lebu	J. E. Robinson.
Corral and Valdivia	G. Roepke Hermanos.
Ancud	Juan Burr.
Calbuco	Thos. Pigott.
Port Montt	Enrique Braemer.

UNITED STATES.

New York	J. Bruce Ismay.
San Francisco	Pacific Mail S.S. Co

SHIPS' WATCHES & BELLS.

The twenty four hours are divided on board ship into seven parts, and the crew is divided into two parts or watches, designated Port and Starboard Watches. Each watch is on duty four hours, excepting between 4 and 8 p.m., when the time is divided into two watches of two hours each, called Dog Watches, by means of which the watches are changed every day, and each watch gets a turn of eight hours' rest at night. *First Watch*, 8 p.m. to midnight ; *Middle Watch*, midnight to 4 a.m. : *Morning Watch*, 4 to 8 a.m. : *Forenoon Watch*, 8 a.m. to noon : *Afternoon Watch*, noon to 4 p.m. : *First Dog Watch*, 4 to 6 p.m. : *Second Dog Watch*, 6 to 8 p.m. The Watches of the Senior Officers in charge of the Steamer's bridge are each of two hours' duration, giving every Officer two hours on duty and four hours off.

1 Bell	12.30 a.m.	
2 Bells	1.00 "	
3 "	1.30 "	
4 "	2.00 "	
5 "	2.30 "	
6 "	3.00 "	
7 "	3.30 "	
8 "	4.00 "	
1 Bell	4.30 "	
2 Bells	5.00 "	
3 "	5.30 "	
4 "	6.00 "	
5 "	6.30 "	
6 "	7.00 "	
7 "	7.30 "	
8 "	8.00 "	
1 Bell	8.30 "	
2 Bells	9.00 "	
3 "	9.30 "	
4 "	10.00 "	
5 "	10.30 "	
6 "	11.00 "	
7 "	11.30 "	
8 "	12.00 noon.	

1 Bell	12.30 p.m.	
2 Bells	1.00 "	
3 "	1.30 "	
4 "	2.00 "	
5 "	2.30 "	
6 "	3.00 "	
7 "	3.30 "	
8 "	4.00 "	
1 Bell	4.30 "	
2 Bells	5.00 "	
3 "	5.30 "	
4 "	6.00 "	
1 Bell	6.30 "	
2 Bells	7.00 "	
3 "	7.30 "	
4 "	8.00 "	
1 Bell	8.30 "	
2 Bells	9.00 "	
3 "	9.30 "	
4 "	10.00 "	
5 "	10.30 "	
6 "	11.00 "	
7 "	11.30 "	
8 "	12.00 night.	

COATS OF ARMS AND FLAGS,

OF THE SEVERAL SOUTH AMERICAN REPUBLICS SERVED BY PACIFIC LINE STEAMERS.

The East Coast of South America.

CHAPTER II.

BRAZILIAN PORTS.

PERNAMBUCO.

Pernambuco, or Recife, as it is called (the latter word meaning reef), is the most important seaport in North Brazil. Its harbour, which can accommodate vessels of the largest tonnage, is formed by the recife, a singular coral reef which borders the shore, more or less from Bahia to Maranham, a distance of nearly a thousand miles.

The commercial port of Pernambuco consists of three divisions, named Recife, San Antonio, and Boa Vista, the first two of which are situated on Sand Banks and connected one with the other by magnificent iron bridges. The business portion of the city is situated in the Recife, which is an old Dutch looking quarter, and presents rather a quaint appearance. The principal feature of the Recife is the Lingueta (landing stage), which faces the open sea. Here are situated all the European houses of business, banks, cable offices, &c., and a greater part of the business is transacted under the shade of the trees on the front, which, being always cool, is used by the merchants and people as a kind of exchange. In general, the town is well built, and there are many lofty houses and comfortable villas constructed with considerable taste, so that Pernambuco bears the appearance of being a very busy and thriving town. The principal streets are the Rua Imperador, Rua Marquex d'Olinda, Rua Nova, Rua de Cadeia, and Rua de Crespo. There are many fine shops and public buildings, which are well worth a visit, the principal among the latter being the Governor's Residence, the Treasury, the Town Hall, the Arsenal, and several Convents and Churches. There is also a fine theatre, at which Italian Opera Companies frequently give performances.

For visitors making a short stay, interesting excursions can be made to Olinda, which is situated on a hill, distant four miles from Pernambuco; at the summit being a fine old Monastery, which is now used as the residence of the Bishop of the Diocese. An extensive view can be obtained here of the surroundings of Pernambuco. Caxanga, an outlying village from the town, may also be visited. Visitors will find an interest in this journey in seeing fields of sugar canes and pine apples, for the latter of which Pernambuco is so celebrated. The above places can easily be reached by the street railway trains, running every hour. There is also a very good service of trams running to the suburbs, to which a visit would prove of interest. Travellers having plenty of time at their disposal, and desirous of more extensive knowledge of Brazil, and those who are interested in ornithological and botanical subjects, will find that a visit to the interior will give them ample opportunity to pursue their favourite studies. Garanhuns, which is about 150 miles from Pernambuco, and situated 2500 feet above the sea level, is well worth a visit, owing to its beautiful cool temperature ; and, besides, it is a great centre for the collection of orchids, of which there are many fine varieties. Coffee is planted freely here, and experts predict a great future for this industry. It is also used as a health resort for people from Pernambuco, and can be reached in eight hours by trains which leave Pernambuco every day. There are good services of trains running into the interior, passing many sugar and cotton plantations, and factories, which, during the crop season, are well worth a visit.

The principal railways of Pernambuco are :—

The Recife and Sao Francisco (Pernambuco) Railway, running South to Una, from which place there is an extension running to Garanhuns.

C

From Una, the Sul Pernambuco Railway runs on to Maceio, an important export town for sugar, hides, &c.

The Great Western of Brazil Railway, running to Timbauba, passes Pao d'Alho and Nazareth; all important towns, where the process of drying and preparing skins is carried on to a great extent.

From Timbauba the diligence can be taken to Pilar, a station on the Conde D'Eu Railway, which runs to Parahyba. This is the only overland route from Pernambuco to Parahyba, and takes about thirty hours.

The principal hotels are :—

The Hotel de Caxanga, recently rebuilt and laid out in the latest style. This Hotel is well situated for travellers who wish to get away from the heat of the town.

Hotel Casa de Banhos, built on the reef itself, is very handy for travellers having business in the town, as the Lingueta can be reached by boat in about five minutes.

There are also a few good English Boarding Houses, full particulars of which can be obtained from the Agents of The Pacific Steam Navigation Co. (Messrs. Wilson, Sons & Co. Ltd.)

Visitors or tourists for the Amazons will find this a very good central port to start from, there being well regulated lines of National steamers running to Manaos three times a month.

The population of Pernambuco is about 150,000.

BAHIA.

The Bay of Bahia, or Bay of All Saints, as it is called, was discovered in 1503 by Americus Vespucius, under the patronage of the King of Portugal, Don Manoel; and is formed on the west by the Island Itaparica, and on the east by the Peninsula on which stands the City of St. Salvador or Bahia.

The entrance to the Bay is much wider than that of Rio, though the bays otherwise will not bear comparison for picturesque effect, Rio Bay being infinitely superior. Bahia Bay is, however, far from being devoid of beauty, and the Coast is bordered by low hills, many of which are well covered with trees.

The approach to the City, which is well situated, is very interesting. The City consists of an upper and a lower town; the means of communication being principally by a lift, an inclined plane, and a well-constructed inclined road, supported for most of its length by arches. The principal part of the lower town is used for commercial purposes, and is not remarkable for its cleanliness.

The upper town, which is built on the cliffs, contains the residential quarters, hotels, and the better class of shops.

The principal hotels are the Hotel Sul Americano (see Advertisement, page 163) Hotel Paris, and Luzo Brazileira.

This City is known as the "City of the Blacks," owing to the great preponderance of blacks over whites. Out of a population of 230,000, there are only about 50,000 white people.

Lovers of birds can obtain great varieties in the markets, one of the principal of which is directly in front of the landing stage.

An interesting trip by tramcar may be made through the upper town to the suburb of Victoria, from the heights of which a charming and extensive view is obtainable. Another pleasant trip is to the fishing village of Rio Vermelho, situated on the Atlantic side of the Peninsula. The journey is made by tramway from the Praça de Palacio (at top of lift) to Campo Grande, where passengers change to a steam tram, which takes them direct to Rio Vermelho.

The return trip can be made by a lower line, which is very picturesque. Passengers, however, should not attempt this excursion unless they have from six to eight hours in port.

The Island Itaparica, opposite to Bahia, is enriched by numerous villages delightfully situated. Its chief town, near the north end, is the general mart of the island, and the rendezvous of all the launches passing through the inlets and creeks of this part of the bay. The island is about 18 miles long and five miles wide on an average. It has a population of about 16,000 souls.

RIO DE JANEIRO.

The City of Rio de Janeiro, which is situated on one of the most beautiful harbours in the world, covers an area of from 8 to 9 square miles, and contains all the buildings and attributes of a large and handsome city. It lies between Castle St. Antonio and Santa Thereza Hills on the South, and St. Bento Conceição and Livramento Hills on the North; and spreads outwards to the West over an extensive low plain.

The harbour is justly celebrated as one of the largest and safest in the world, and the coast line is exceedingly irregular on both sides, and picturesquely broken into many smaller lagoon-like bays. The entrance, which is about one

mile in width, is from a southerly direction, with the Islands of Pai and Mãi on the right and Ilha Raza (with its lighthouse) and a number of other semi-barren Islands on the left. The editors of the *Rio News* in their handbook of Rio, which is no doubt the best guide to that city obtainable, describes the Bay of Rio de Janeiro as follows:—

> "A miniature summer sea, sleeping within the embrace of granite mountain chains, upon whose bosom rest a hundred fairy isles, and around whose shores dimple a hundred tiny bays. A fairer scene eyes

never beheld. Near at hand are the bare grey peaks which cluster about the entrance as though to beat back the ocean storms, while in the distance are the ever-green slopes and rugged profile of the far-famed Organ Mountain."

"No matter," says Mr. J. W. Wells, in his *3,000 Miles Through Brazil*, "how many times a traveller may approach this shore, it will always impress and delight him ; it is ever changing, always different, for, from varied points of view, the rocky mountains assume different forms; they may be distorted in appearance by the clouds of mist that envelop or hide them in the early mornings; or they may be bare and bright, and glimmer in the fierce light of day ; or become rosy and tinted with manifold colours with the rays of the setting sun."

"The Bay of Naples, the Golden Horn of Constantinople, and the Bay of Rio," to quote from *Brazil and*

the Brazilians, by the Rev. James C. Fletcher and D. P. Kidder, "are always mentioned by the travelled tourist as pre-eminently worthy to be classed together for their extent and for the beauty and sublimity of their scenery. The first two, however, must yield the palm to the last-named magnificent sheet of water, which, in a climate of perpetual summer, is enclosed within the ranges of singularly picturesque mountains, and is dotted with verdure-covered islands of the tropics."

One is struck on entering the Bay with the beauty of the mountainous coast line, which, taken *en masse*, forms a huge resemblance of the human figure, and has thus earned for itself the appellation of the "Sleeping Giant."

The most famous of the numerous peaks, is the Sugar Loaf (Pão de Assucar), which rises abruptly from the sea at the entrance to the harbour to a height of 1,363 feet.

In the front of the Sugar Loaf, but separated from it, is a fort, perched on a large rock rising above the bay. There is a second fort in the centre of the entrance, and a third on the right side.

The City of Rio contains quite a number of objects of interest, and there are many excursions which may be conveniently made in a few hours by tram and rail. The public squares and gardens are justly renowned, and are of rare beauty and interest. The most celebrated of these lies upon the water front at the Caes Pharoux landing place, and is surrounded by public buildings. The prettiest garden in the City however is the Passeio Publico, situated

on the shore of the bay and facing the entrance to the harbour.

The population of the City and municipal district of Rio de Janeiro is at present calculated to be 500,000.

In 1754 the first coffee tree was planted in the district, and Coffee is now the chief product of the country, mainly in the provinces of Rio Minas Geraes and São Paulo. The duties on imports are heavy, and trade is much hampered by strict quarantine regulations. The suburbs of Rio are very picturesque, the best perhaps being those which lie to the south-west, namely, Cattete, Larangeiras, Botafogo and Gavea. The suburb of Tijuca is also very beautiful, and should certainly be visited.

As respects hotel accommodation, travellers are advised to consult the Agents of The Pacific S. N. Co., Messrs. Wilson, Sons & Co., Limited. The best are probably the Grande Hotel Metropole at Larangeiras (see advertisement page 164), Carson's, the Hotel Estrangeiros

in the Cattete, Hotel Whyte at Tijuca, and Hotel Internacional at Santa Thereza.

The city and suburbs are well supplied with tramway lines, nearly all running from points on or near the Rua do Ouvidor.

The following are probably the most interesting trips which travellers having but a short time at their disposal can make, viz. :—

    1.—Botanical Gardens (fare each way, Rs. 300), about six miles from the city, are easily reached by tram from the Largo de Carioca. Green trams, marked "Jardim," leave the Largo every 15 minutes, and put the passenger down at the gate of the gardens, after a journey of about an hour.

The chief attraction is the avenue of Royal Palms, about 550 yards in length. The gardens, which are picturesquely situated, can be thoroughly explored in about three-quarters of an hour. This trip may with advantage be extended to the terminus of the tram line at the Gavea village, which nestles at the foot of the Carioca Mountain range. From the end of the tram line it is about 20 minutes to the top of the hill, from which fine views can be obtained in several directions.

2.—Corcovado Mountain (2,275 feet) is easily accessible by tram and train in about three hours. A yellow tram, marked "Larangeiras," leaves the Largo de Carioca every 15 minutes, and passes the railway station, from which the ascent is made by train. Trains leave on week days at 6-30 a.m., 8 a.m., 11 a.m., 2 p.m., 5-15 p.m., and 8 p.m., while on Sundays there are extra trains at 9-30 a.m., 12-30 p.m., and 3-30 p.m. The tram ride occupies about three quarters of an hour, and the ascent by train about one hour and a half. Two-thirds of the way up stands a first-class hotel, where visitors will find excellent accommodation at reasonable rates. The scenery during the ascent is varied, as the train passes through the tropical forest which clothes the sides of the mountain. The view from the top embraces the city and suburbs, the bay and shipping, the open sea, and the wooded slopes of the Tijuca Mountains behind, the panorama being considered one of the finest in the world. The tram fare is Rs. 200 each way, and the railway ticket (return) costs Rs. 2,000.

3.—Tijuca comprises a village with well-found hotels situated in an upland valley between two ranges of mountains. Beautiful walks and drives are found in every direction, as the surrounding forest is preserved by the Government, and is laid out in fine gravel walks, which wind amongst the mountains in all directions. There are also several waterfalls worth a visit. Tijuca is reached by tram and diligence. Trams leave the Largo de S. Francisco de Paulo every 15 minutes, the journey to the starting point of the diligence occupying one hour and ten minutes, and the fare being Rs. 300 each way. Diligences leave at 8.10 a.m., 3.10 p.m. and 5.15 p.m. on week days, and at 7.30 a.m., 9.30 a.m., 11.30 a.m., 3.30 p.m. and 5.30 p.m. on Sundays, the fare either way being Rs. 1500. The ascent of the principal peak of the range (3,300 feet) can be made in two hours on foot from the village.

4.—Petropolis, the City of Peter—so named because it owes its foundation and development to Emperor

Pedro II.—a town of about 20,000 inhabitants, and formerly the residence of the Court during the days of the Empire, lies at a level of 2,000 feet above the sea, amongst the Organ Mountains, 45 miles from the city. A screw steamer starts at 4 p.m. on week days, and 7 a.m. on Sundays, carrying passengers to the top of the Bay, where a train awaits them to complete the journey, which occupies altogether about two hours and a half. The fare is Rs. 12,000 return. Passengers cannot return the same day.

5.—Nova Friburgo lies at a height of 3,000 feet above the sea, and is situated in the Organ Mountains, about 70 miles from Rio. It is reached by train starting from the S. Anna terminus of the Leopoldina Railway. Trains leave twice a day, but the return journey cannot be performed on the day of starting. A return ticket available for three days costs Rs. 12,000.

6.—Paqueta: An island lying 7 miles from the city of Rio de Janeiro, and about the middle of the Bay, is a favourite suburban residence. The island can be easily explored in about two hours, and the excursionist will meet with some very pretty nooks. The shore is lined with cocoa-nut palms, and has an ideal tropical appearance. Boats leave Rio at

9 a.m. and 6 p.m., the fare being Rs. 500 each way on week days, and Rs. 1,000 each way on Sundays. Return boats leave the island at 8 a.m., 1 p.m. and 6.30 p.m.

7.—There are various small gardens about the city of Rio tastefully laid out. The principal are the Passeio Publico, reached by any tram from the Largo de Carioca. This garden has a promenade facing the Bay, and is altogether a shady retreat, where a few hours may be pleasantly whiled away.

Jardim da Praça da Acclammação is reached by any tram from the Largo de S. Francisco de Paulo, but has no special features worthy of mention.

8.—Tram Rides: Besides those mentioned to the Botanical Gardens and Tijuca, there is one other specially deserving of mention. The intending passenger takes in the Rua Primeiro de Marco a narrow guage tram marked "Riachuelo," which will set him down at the "Plano Inclinado" or lift, by which the ascent is made to S. Thereza Hill, one of the spurs of the Corcovado Mountain. At the top of the lift a tram waits, which follows a road cut out of the side of the mountain. The terminus of this tram is at Sylvestre, a station of the Corcovado Railway, at a height of about 600 feet above the sea level. The various views of the city, bay, and surrounding mountains, will amply repay this trip, to say nothing of the wealth of tropical foliage through which the route passes. This trip occupies altogether about four hours. The fare is Rs. 100 in the first tram, while for the lift and second tram a return ticket costing Rs. 800 is taken at the lift station. Trams run at frequent intervals throughout the day.

The following list of sailings from Rio will be of service to passengers bound to the Southern Ports of Brazil.

NATIONAL LINE OF COASTING STEAMERS.

(Companhia Nacional de Navegação Costeira.)

This Company possesses a fleet of first-class passenger steamers, which leave Rio de Janeiro every Saturday for Porto Alegre, viâ Paranaguá, Desterro, Rio Grande and Pelotas.

Destination.	TIME TABLE.		FARES.	
	Arrival.	Departure.	1st Class.	3rd Class.
			Rs.	Rs.
Paranaguá	Monday	Monday	65.000	25.000
Desterro	Tuesday	Wednesday	75.000	38.000
Rio Grande	Thursday	Thursday	140.000	50.000
Pelotas	Friday	Friday	145.000	54.000
Porto Alegre	Saturday	Saturday	165.000	63.000

Return Tickets, valid for three months, are also sold

for Rio Grande (240.000), Pelotas (250.000), and Porto Alegre (290.000).

Passengers for São Paulo will see from the following time table of the Brazilian Central Railway (Estrado de Ferro Central) that the trains leave Rio at 6-15 a.m., arriving in São Paulo at 8-40 p.m., stopping at the Barra do Pirahy and Taubaté, the former for breakfast and the latter for dinner. Twenty minutes are allowed for each meal, but this time generally develops into half an hour.

Trains start every day from Rio de Janeiro for São Paulo.

TIME TABLE.

Destination	Arrival	Departure	Destination	Arrival	Departure
Rio de Janeiro	–	6-15 a.m.	São Paulo	–	5-00 a.m.
Barra do Pirahy	8-45 a.m.	*9-05 a.m.	Taubaté	9-23 a.m.°	9-42 a.m.
Taubaté	3-40 p.m.	†4-00 p.m.	Barra do Pirahy	4-18 p.m.†	4-35 p.m.
São Paulo	8-40 p.m.	—	Rio de Janeiro	7-00 p.m.	—

* 20 minutes for Breakfast.   † 20 minutes for Dinner.

Fares to São Paulo.

1st Class.	*2nd* Class.	*1st* Class Return Ticket.
Rs. 29.620	Rs. 15.600	Rs. 44.600

CHAPTER III.

THE RIVER PLATE.

MONTE VIDEO, URUGUAY, ARGENTINE REPUBLIC, PARAGUAY.

The River Plate, so called on account of its passing in its course the territories from which the Indians derived their supplies of silver, can scarcely be designated a river, it being, more properly speaking, the broad estuary formed by the waters of the Rivers Paraná and Uruguay.

The width of the estuary from Monte Video to Point las Piedras, on the Argentine coast, is 53 miles, whilst at its mouth, say from Cape St. Mary, in Uruguay, to Cape St. Anthony, in the province of Buenos Ayres, the width is 150 miles.

On entering the bay, which is very much exposed, a splendid view is obtained of the "glistening domes, cupolas, and spires of Monte Video."

MONTE VIDEO.

This City, which was officially created in 1724, is the seat of government and capital of the Republic of Uruguay, and was originally built at the narrow end of a small peninsula at the mouth of the Plate. The town, however,

has of late years rapidly increased, and now extends to the mainland. The population of the City is about 180,000. The City is named after the "Cerro" or mount, which is the most prominent object on entering the bay. Part of the shore of the bay has been enclosed by an embankment, which forms an excellent promenade. The City possesses many objects of interest to the traveller, and the several public resorts are readily reached by means of tramways, with which the City is intersected. The Cathedral should be visited. At night time the leading streets are lighted by electricity, and are particularly brilliant and interesting.

The principal exports are hides, horns, tallow, and wool, and the chief industry is cattle rearing. In the neighbourhood of Monte Video, and on the River Uruguay, there are a number of saladeros, including in the latter vicinity the establishment belonging to the Liebig Extract of Meat Company at Fray Bentos. This employs a very large number of men, and loads at its own wharves 80 to 100 vessels a year with its own produce for Europe. We learn from the statistics published by the Uruguayan Consul that the number of cattle killed at the saladeros each year often exceeds 600,000, of which nearly 150,000 are used for Liebig's Extract; and, in addition, a large number of sheep, and 60,000 to 80,000 mares are killed annually.

URUGUAY, officially known as the Oriental Republic of the Uruguay, is familiarly termed the "Banda Oriental," from its geographical position on the left bank of the River Uruguay. The area of the Republic is 186,920 square kilometres, and the population about 700,000. The climate of the Republic is proverbial, not only on account of the mildness of the air, but also for its salubrity. The Consul-General, London, has issued an excellent pamphlet on the resources of the Republic, which may be had "gratis" on written application to any of the Consulates of the Republic in Great Britain, Ireland, and the British Possessions.

The towns of **Paysandú** and **Salto**, which are situated on the river Uruguay, can be reached by steamers sailing at 6 p.m. from Monte Video almost every evening; or by train leaving at 8.50 p.m. on Tuesdays, Thursdays and Saturdays.

The scenery up the river Uruguay is very beautiful in some parts.

The best hotels in Monte Video are the "Hotel Oriental" (see Advertisement) and the "Hotel des Pyramides;" and the Restaurant Charpentier is justly famed for its excellent cuisine.

BUENOS AYRES.

Passengers for Buenos Ayres are conveyed from Monte Video by the steamers of the La Platense Company. These steamers are luxuriously fitted, and form an excellent service. They sail from Monte Video at 5 to 6 p.m., according to the season of the year, and arrive at Buenos Ayres at 5 to 6 a.m. the following day.

The city of Buenos Ayres—which aspires to the title of the "Athens of South America"—extends for a distance of four miles along the right bank of the La Plata, and

covers an area of about six square miles. It has a
population of 600,000 inhabitants.

The best hotels are the Royal, the Grand, and the
Britannia; the last-named under English management, all
being recommended. The Royal Hotel is considered the
most comfortable, and the Britannia the most economical.
Visitors to Buenos Ayres, however, can arrange to
stay in furnished houses (casas amuebladas), in which
comfortable rooms may be obtained at reasonable prices,
the occupants being left to make their own arrangements
as to food. There are a large number of such houses, the
addresses of which can be obtained from the Pacific
Company's agents.

There are many spacious and imposing buildings in
this city and its suburbs, and also numerous places of

amusement. The city is well lighted, and looks extremely pretty. There are a number of outdoor recreation grounds, and probably Palermo Park—which contains a zoological collection—will be found the most interesting. In summer it is very popular as the fashionable drive or Rotten Row of Buenos Ayres. Calle Florida is known as *the* street of Buenos Ayres, but this honour is now being disputed by the new Avenida de Mayo, which intersects the city from

south to north. For the favourite holiday resorts on the numerous fertile islands formed by the River Parana at Tigre, numerous steam launches and rowing boats are available. The suburbs of Adrogué, Temperley and Flores are pretty, and have a large population of English residents. Belgrano, nearer the city, is much preferred by English and

Germans. At Adrogué a very good hotel is established, and is favourably spoken of.

Railway communication with the various Provinces is general and the tariffs are moderate. Luxurious sleeping and dining cars are attached to all trains going long distances. The principal railway lines (all of which are under English management) are as follows :—

The "GREAT SOUTHERN" runs from Buenos Ayres away to the South as far as BAHIA BLANCA, a rapidly-advancing port, and MAR DEL PLATA, the popular Argentine Brighton, where excellent bathing and good hotel accommodation are to be had. TANDIL is a point of interest on this line from the noted immense rocking stone in its vicinity. Fares: Bahia Blanca, £1 15s 0d; Mar del Plata, £1 5s 0d.

The "BUENOS AYRES AND ROSARIO RAILWAY," as its name implies, connects the capital with the Port of Rosario, the second of importance in the Republic, and from which the bulk of the wheat grown in the Colonies of Santa Fé is shipped. The journey to Rosario occupies about nine hours, and is made comfortably in luxurious trains fitted with dining and sleeping cars; the fare is about £1. This Railway service extends over a large tract of country connecting with the immense plantations of sugar cane in Tucuman and the Northern Provinces.

The "CENTRAL ARGENTINE RAILWAY" competes with the Rosario Railway Company for the traffic between Buenos Ayres and Rosario; this competition has the effect of providing two excellent services, both highly recommended. The terminus of this Company is the city of **Cordova**, a distance of about 257 miles from Rosario, and reached in about 15 hours. The fare from Rosario is about £3.

Cosquin, a village in the mountains near Cordova, is a favourite resort of the Argentine holiday seeker, and is recommended for its healthy climate.

The "BUENOS AYRES AND PACIFIC RAILWAY," in connection with the Argentine Great Western and Trans-Andine Lines, is that by which travellers are conveyed overland to Valparaiso. The terminus of these lines, Mendoza, nestling at the foot of the Andes, is well worth a visit, and its climate is recommended by the faculty for consumptives and sufferers from other lung complaints. The Province of Mendoza is the vineyard of the country.

A very enjoyable trip can be made from Buenos Ayres to **Asuncion**, the capital of the **Republic of Paraguay**, in five to six days by the steamers of the Platense Flotilla Company, Limited, at a cost of about £14, return. The river service is an excellent one, the steamers being well provided with all modern conveniences and an excellent table; while the views on the voyage cannot be excelled, the river Paraná being one of the finest waterways in the world.

Paraguay, the land of oranges, is particularly interesting to the traveller; the customs of the Paraguayans being decidedly primitive, and the vegetation tropical.

At **San Bernardino**, two hours from Asuncion, there is a German Colony with excellent country hotels at very moderate prices—prices considerably lower than in Europe. Indeed, living in Paraguay is very cheap, the paper currency there being at a discount of 600 per cent. as compared with gold; the sovereign thus being worth 30 dollars. Even Argentine paper enjoys a premium of 90 per cent.

CHAPTER IV.

STRAITS OF MAGELLAN.

After three and a half to four days' run from Monte Video we enter the famous Straits, discovered by the great navigator Magellan in 1520.

When approaching the Straits, and at a distance of about 20 miles from Cape Virgins, what appears to be a double horizon is seen, the phenomenon being, no doubt, due to the level character of the land. Cape Virgins (135 feet high) commands the North-Eastern entrance to the Straits, and is visible at a distance of from 20 to 25 miles. The South-Eastern point is named Cape Espiritu Santo, the distance between the two Capes being about 22 miles. Cape Virgins and Cape Espiritu Santo have certain points of resemblance, both being marked with white cliffs, and both having low shingle points connected with them, which reduce the width of the entrance to 14 miles from point to point.

Espiritu Santo is 190 feet high, and is the seaward termination of a range of hills, varying from 200 to a little over 900 feet in height, which extends N.E. and S.W. at the back of the promontories which form the Narrows, as far as Cape Boqueron, opposite Port Famine. The highest part of this range terminates in Gap Peak, which rises 925

TRACK CHART
OF THE
RAITS OF MAGELLAN

feet above the sea, between the First and Second Narrows. Cape Espiritu Santo does not show as an extreme until inside the Straits, but if seen from seaward its appearance is remarkable and unmistakable, as being the highest part of a line of white cliffs, indented by bays which, at a distance, give it the appearance of having had gaps cut in it.

From Cape Virgins to the passage known as the First Narrows, the land on the North side is more undulating than at the Cape, and is covered with grass. The entrance to the Narrows resembles a large gateway. There is a rise of water here of about 50 feet at spring tides. These Narrows are 9 miles long by 2 miles wide navigable.

Proceeding from the First for a distance of 18 miles and through Philip Bay, we reach the Second Narrows. These are 12 miles long, and vary in width from 3 to 4 miles navigable, and there is a rise in the water at spring tides of 23 feet. The course through these Narrows is fairly direct until the point at Cape St. Vincent (so called from its similarity to Cape St. Vincent in the South of Portugal) is reached. From this Cape for some 12 to 15 miles the direction taken is, owing to a number of shoals and small islands, very circuitous. Thence to Sandy Point a fairly direct course is taken. In clear weather, long before Sandy Point is reached, indeed before a vessel gets through the Second Narrows, the high mountains on Dawson Islands

feet above the sea, between the First and Second Narrows. Cape Espiritu Santo does not show as an extreme until inside the Straits, but if seen from seaward its appearance is remarkable and unmistakable, as being the highest part of a line of white cliffs, indented by bays which, at a distance, give it the appearance of having had gaps cut in it.

From Cape Virgins to the passage known as the First Narrows, the land on the North side is more undulating than at the Cape, and is covered with grass. The entrance to the Narrows resembles a large gateway. There is a rise of water here of about 50 feet at spring tides. These Narrows are 9 miles long by 2 miles wide navigable.

Proceeding from the First for a distance of 18 miles and through Philip Bay, we reach the Second Narrows. These are 12 miles long, and vary in width from 3 to 4 miles navigable, and there is a rise in the water at spring tides of 23 feet. The course through these Narrows is fairly direct until the point at Cape St. Vincent (so called from its similarity to Cape St. Vincent in the South of Portugal) is reached. From this Cape for some 12 to 15 miles the direction taken is, owing to a number of shoals and small islands, very circuitous. Thence to Sandy Point a fairly direct course is taken. In clear weather, long before Sandy Point is reached, indeed before a vessel gets through the Second Narrows, the high mountains on Dawson Islands and Mount San Felipe will be seen, forming an apparent barrier blocking up the passage, and over the latter the summit of Mount Tarn stands out in bold relief against the sky. The view presented by these mountains from the anchorage off Sandy Point is a magnificent one. After passing the Second Narrows, Elizabeth Island, so named by Sir Francis Drake, comes into sight. At Cape Negro, about 14 miles from Sandy Point, is seen the last Southerly spur of the Cordilleras, which run along the Coast and join the main ridge beyond Sandy Point. All these spurs are clothed with beech forests and thick underwood of the Magnolia species.

Sandy Point (Punta Arenas), which is situated at a distance of about 120 miles from Cape Virgins, and is officially known by the Chilians, to whom it belongs, as "La Colonia de Magellanes," was simply a convict settlement up to the year 1877, when it was disestablished in consequence of a revolt of the convicts and its great distance from the seat of Government—Santiago. Since 1877 the town has largely developed, and the population composed of all nationalities now sums up to about 9,000. Sandy Point may be considered the most Southern town in the world. It has now

five hotels, three churches, a plaza, and numerous streets, the latter taking a right-angular form, and extending, in some instances, from half a mile to a mile. It possesses a Resident Governor, a Municipality has recently been formed, and in general terms it may be stated that the Colony is in a most flourishing condition and likely to make rapid progress. Its growing prosperity is due chiefly to the rearing of sheep and cattle, which goes on both in

Chile and in Tierra del Fuego, and it is the centre for wool shipments in the Straits of Magellan. Leaving Sandy Point we reach, at a distance to the South of about 25 miles, Port Famine, at which a Colony was established by Sarmiento in 1580. On his return eight years subsequently, it was discovered that nearly all the Colonists had died from starvation; hence the name—Port Famine.

At this part there is a complete change in the whole appearance of the Straits. The mountainous district is now approached. Here we have snow-clad mountain ranges running up to 2,000 feet in height on both sides of the Straits. Proceeding onwards to a point named San Isidro the scenery becomes grand. To the South, some 40 miles distant, Mount Sarmiento comes into view.

Mount Sarmiento and Mount Buckland form the two most conspicuous peaks in the high mass of mountains running along the South side of the Gabriel Channel. The first, situated at the South-East Angle of Magdalen Sound, is 7,300 feet high, and rising from a broad base terminates in two peaked summits about a quarter of a mile asunder. From the Northward they appear very much like the crater of a volcano, but when viewed from the Westward the two peaks are in line and the volcanic resemblance ceases. Mount Sarmiento is the most remarkable mountain in Magellan Straits; but from the climate and its being clothed with perpetual snow, it is almost always enveloped in condensed vapour. During a low temperature, however, particularly with a North-East or South-East wind, when the sky is often cloudless, it is exposed to view and presents a magnificent appearance.

The late Professor Darwin, in his "Voyage of H.M.S. 'Beagle,'" writes regarding Mount Sarmiento, as follows :—

"In the morning we were delighted by seeing the veil of mist gradually rise from Sarmiento and display it to our view. Its base for about an eighth of its total height is clothed by dusky woods, and above this a field of snow extends to the summit. These vast piles of snow, which never melt and seem destined to last as long as the world holds together, present a noble and even sublime spectacle. The outline of the mountain was admirably clear and defined. Owing to the abundance of light reflected from the white and glittering surface no shadows were cast on any part, and those lines which intersected the sky could alone be distinguished : hence the mass stood out in the boldest relief. Several Glaciers descended in a winding course from the upper great expanse of snow to the sea coast ; they may be likened to great frozen Niagaras, and perhaps these cataracts of blue ice are full as beautiful as the moving ones of water."

Mount Buckland, on the West shore of Fitton harbour is, by estimation, about 4,000 feet high. It is a pyramidal block of slate, with a sharp pointed apex, and covered with perpetual snow. Between these mountains the summit of the range is occupied by an extensive glacier, the constant dissolution of which feeds innumerable cascades which pour large bodies of water down the rocky precipices overhanging the Southern shore of Gabriel Channel.

Proceeding onwards from San Isidro, some 13 miles, Cape Froward is passed. This cape, in latitude 53.33 S., is

the Southernmost headland of the Continent proper of South America, and can be passed close to by the steamer. It is 1,200 feet high, and above it rises the great snow-clad peak of Mount Victoria, 2,900 feet. The course now taken is in a North-Westerly direction for some 25 miles, the channel being about 4 miles wide. It then narrows to about ¾ of a mile in one part. The mountains on either side are forest-clad up to an elevation of 700 feet more or less, and are always capped with snow.

Sometimes when steamers are passing through the narrow reaches Westward of Cape Froward small canoes glide out from some of the openings. Each canoe apparently contains a family of Indians from Tierra del Fuego, as, usually, there is a man, with one or two women and children. There is always a fire alight at the bottom of the canoe, and there are likewise three or four dogs. The Indians have very little clothing on—occasionally sealskins, sometimes an old blanket or coat or vest that some charitable or kindly-disposed passenger may have given them. The women row the canoe with primitive paddles, and the man holds up one or two skins for barter. When approaching a steamer they call out, "Galleta, tabac," the Spanish words for biscuit and tobacco.

The Fuegians are possibly the lowest type of savage in the world; though, since 1830—when Captain R. Fitzroy, of H.M.S. "Beagle," brought four of the natives to England, and, after partially educating them restored them to their own country—repeated efforts have been made to civilize them. Much credit is due to the untiring efforts of Missionaries in this direction, and to their persistency in the face of immense difficulties. These Missionaries have, to a great extent, acquired the language and reduced it to writing, and, in addition to inculcating the Christian doctrine, they are endeavouring to teach the natives habits of industry and the value of agriculture. We extract the following

E

description of the Fuegians from one of the South American Missionary Society's publications :—

"The Fuegians may be roughly divided into Canoe Indians and Foot Indians, the latter occupying the main island. The foot Indians are a superior race to the canoe Indians, more akin to those of Patagonia. They rarely use canoes, but live on the sports of the chase.

"On the East coast the natives use a guanaco skin as a cloak ; on the West sealskins are used. Among the central tribes the men, for the most part, have either an otter skin or a sealskin as a partial protection for the body ;

but some are to be found entirely destitute of clothing. Polygamy exists certainly amongst some of the tribes, and probably among all. Among the different tribes there seems to be no Government or chief. They are a thriftless people, with no domestic animals excepting dogs; not given to tilling the ground, and dependent, in the case of the canoe Indians, on fish and fungus; in that of the foot Indians, on the skilful use of the bow and arrow. The whale is a great boon to them, for they feed on the blubber and manufacture the bones into spear heads and other instruments of hunting, and make fishing lines of plaited sinews. Yet these natives could not procure a whale for themselves, but are indebted to the swordfish for harassing and driving ashore these monsters of the deep."

Writing on the subject of the physical features and zoology of Tierra del Fuego, Darwin says:—

"The country may be described as a mountainous land partly submerged in the sea, so that deep inlets and bays occupy the place where valley should exist. The mountain sides, except on the exposed Western coast, are covered from the water's edge upwards by one great forest. The trees reach to an elevation of between 1000 to 1500 feet, and are succeeded by a band of peat, with minute alpine plants, and this again is succeeded by the line of perpetual snow. Level land is scarcely to be found. The zoology of Tierra del Fuego is very poor. Of mammalia, besides whales and seals, there are one bat, a kind of mouse, two true mice, two foxes, a sea otter, the guanaco, and a deer. Most of these animals inhabit only the drier eastern parts of the country

We now come to Crooked Reach, the entrance to which is formed by a narrow and circuitous channel, and as the Reach is approached there appears to be no outlet, and the ship seems to be locked in on all sides by high mountains. The scenery here is wild and magnificent.

After leaving Crooked Reach the direction taken is comparatively straight for a number of miles along what might practically be called an ocean canal, and the scenery on both sides is of the grandest—numerous glaciers and the scoriated mountains with their snow-clad peaks forming, in the sunlight, a picture which is both dazzling and awe-inspiring. The views given in this book convey but a poor idea of the magnificence of this scenery.

Mr. R. W. Coppinger, in his book "Cruise of the 'Alert,'" says in describing Glacier Bay—"The land here was low and flat, covered with dense forest and bounded on either side by precipitous lofty cliffs, whose smooth faces exhibited planings and scorings due to the abrading action of old glaciers;" and, after landing, and passing through the forest to the moraine at the foot of the glacier, he writes:— "It was a strange sight standing in the middle of this terminal moraine to see, on the one hand, a fresh evergreen forest abounding in the most delicate ferns and mosses and on the other a huge mass of cold, blue-veined ice which was slowly and irresistibly gouging its passage downwards to the sea."

After about four hours' steaming from Crooked Reach the Straits begin to widen; and, from the gentle movement of the vessel, it becomes apparent that the ocean is being approached. Two or three hours later the vessel enters the Pacific Ocean at a point called Cape Pillar, and proceeds to her destination—Valparaiso—calling en route at the Ports of Coronel and Talcahuano.

The distance in a straight line from Cape Virgins to Cape Pillar does not exceed 240 miles, but the projection of Brunswick Peninsula adds about 70 miles to this distance by water. Cape Pillar, the South point of the Western entrance of Magellan Straits, is a high Cape, showing from the Eastward as a double nipple. The Eastern and higher one belongs to a mountain from which the Cape springs, but the Western one is a kind of tower, and is of a form to

which the name "pillar" is applicable. The extremity,
common to the Straits and to the Pacific Ocean, is a large
detached rock, which shows the disposition of the strata of
which it and the Cape are formed. That part of the Cape
which is washed by the waters of the Straits presents a
round hill, not very high ; while the Western part, exposed
to the force of the Pacific Ocean, exhibits large excavations
made by the sea in the rock. The Eastern peak is 1,395
feet high, and the Western 1,287.

Most of the land in South Patagonia has been taken
up in lease-holdings from the Government of Chili; the
largest area which an individual is allowed to have being
20,000 hectares, say 49,425 acres. Sheep farming is the
principal industry, but cattle and horses are also reared.
The principal of these lease-holdings have been taken up by
Englishmen and Scotchmen, whose capital in the aggregate

will amount to more than £150,000. A flock of 10,000 sheep is reckoned as a small one. There is now one combined holding representing 280,000 hectares, and which extends into the Argentine Republic, and contains a flock of 130,000 sheep. In this instance the operations commenced in 1885.

Patagonia was first visited by Englishmen in 1578. Sir Francis Drake in that year anchored in Seal Bay—probably a little to the South of Port Desire.

In regard to Patagonia we cannot do better than give the following extract from Mr. E. W. White's estimable book " Cameos from the Silver Land ":—

"Patagon is a Spanish word augmentative of 'pata,' a paw, and therefore signifies 'large-pawed,' a term applied by the early Spaniards to the Indians of that region when they first beheld them with feet swathed in Guanaco-skins. Patagonia then is the land of the large-pawed. Starting from the Rio Negro, its northern limit, to the Straits of Magellan, from the Andes to the Atlantic this triangle has an area of 372,815 square miles, into which Great Britain and Ireland, France, Denmark, Holland and Belgium could be packed; inhabited by numerous tribes of Indians numbering perhaps 25,000, of which the chief is that of the **Tehuelches**, but it is very probable that all these various families have a common descent from the Araucanians of Southern Chili, whom the Spaniards were never able to subdue, and whose language bears the relation of mother-tongue to all their manifold dialects.

"The story books relate that the Patagonians are of extraordinary stature, and some of the tribes are so, but they are chiefly remarkable for enormous busts, and fleshy

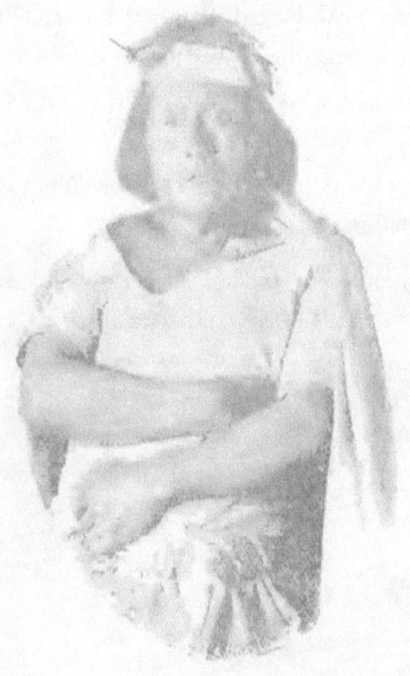

features which, laid over projecting maxillaries and square mandibles, give immense breadth and solidity to the face. The upper limbs are of great power and size, but the lower do not correspond to the bulk of the trunk. Thus seen on horseback, they appear **veritable Titans**; an impression which inspection afoot, although it subdues, yet cannot altogether dispel, as they are undoubtedly very large men, who strike the beholder rather for their extreme breadth and fleshiness than exalted stature; which, however, not uncommonly does reach six feet and upwards. These huge Macropods—with hair long, dank, straight and jet black; eyes so dark that they shed even over the sclerotic a rufous tint; teeth superlatively white, probably the result of drinking saline waters; complexion a dark-ruddy brown, and features the reverse of ferocious—impress one, on the whole, more as good-natured giants than savage Indians."

The number of Indians mentioned by Mr. White would now be more correctly stated as about 10,000.

The West Coast of South America.

CHAPTER V.

COLOMBIA.

The British Minister and Consul-General of Colombia, Mr. George F. B. Jenner, recently reported to the Foreign Office respecting this Republic as follows:—

"The position occupied on the South American Continent by the Republic of Colombia is a highly favourable one. Her coast-line measures 3,400 miles, of which 1,600 are on the Pacific and 1,800 on the Atlantic Ocean. Her possession of the Isthmus of Panama constitutes her the guardian of the future great thoroughfare of the commerce between the two oceans. The aspect of the country is singularly picturesque. The grand chain of the Andes divides into three ranges as it pursues its southern course on entering Colombian territory; forming in all directions table lands at various elevations, and deep and fertile valleys. The scenery is diversified by primeval forests and impenetrable thickets, green and fertile prairies, and vast extents of land suitable for cultivation. Innumerable streams water the country, flowing in every direction in a silver network. The greater portion of the soil is of exceeding richness; and, owing to the great differences of temperature, depending upon the elevation, in some part or other of the country, all the products of the most-favoured zones can be cultivated with advantage. In the hot region, on the coast and in the valleys, coffee, cocoa, bananas, and most varieties of palms, the sugar-cane, indigo, cotton, tobacco, vanilla, and other spices, maize, rice and a number of fruits and medicinal plants grow with the greatest luxuriance. In the temperate regions of the highlands wheat, barley, oats, potatoes, flax, and most edible vegetables flourish under proper care. The forests abound in valuable timber and dyewoods, indiarubber, quinine, sarsaparilla, ipecacuanha, and many other useful drugs. Orchids and other flowers of especial beauty and brilliancy of colour are widely distributed. The birds and insects are equally varied in beauty and equally abundant. In the mineral kingdom the wealth of the Colombian Republic is exceptionally great both in the useful and the precious metals. Colombia, however, with its mountains teeming with mineral wealth, and its plains and valleys of luxuriant soil, has not been endowed by nature with many navigable rivers or safe harbours, by means of which her valuable products may be conveyed to the outer world, and there exchanged for the commodities necessary in the present era of civilisation."

The Pacific Steam Cº Works on Mario Isº 1860

PANAMA was one of the first of the Spanish Settlements in South America, having been founded in 1518, from which time, till the fall of the Spanish dominion, it held a position of considerable importance, as it was by this route that communication was principally maintained between Europe and the richly productive Colonies of the Pacific. The Spanish treasure fleet periodically visited the port to land its bullion for transport over the Isthmus to Porto Bello and re-shipment to Spain. The present is, however, situated three miles to the West of the original port, which latter was destroyed in 1670.

After the retirement of the Spaniards from the Pacific the town fell into decay, and did not again figure until the building of the railway across the Isthmus to Colon, in 1855, gave it back some of its former importance; and this was still more increased by the commencement of the Panama Canal Works in 1881. In January, 1887, the population of the Department was said to amount to 250,000, but at the cessation of the works, in 1889, many thousands of people left the Isthmus, and at present Panama proper has not more than some 15,000 inhabitants.

The port is situated at the upper extremity of the Gulf of Panama, the city itself being built on a narrow tongue of land stretching into the sea, and at the foot of a steep conical hill called Mount Ancon. It is fairly well and solidly built in the more modern parts, and in its general appearance is somewhat more European than other towns on the Coast. There are a fine square and gardens, a cathedral, and several sightly and substantial buildings, as well as two or three fair hotels, such as—

The Grand Hotel...(in the Central Square)...pension $5 per day and upward.
The Marine Hotel...(at the landing steps) ..   " $3
The Commercial Hotel   "   "   "

The Bay of Panama is one of the most charming spots in the Pacific; the conformation of its shores, clothed to the water's edge with tropical vegetation, and the beautiful arrangement of the luxuriant islets dotted here and there in the Bay, present a picture certainly beautiful. It is here that the extensive Pearl Fisheries, which gave to Panama so much of its fame, were formerly carried on, and from this one of the groups still bears the name of the Pearl Islands.

Steamers anchor off Flamenco Island, which is distant about three miles from the town, and is said to be the most healthy spot in Central America. From the anchorage the City presents a somewhat imposing appearance; the churches, houses, and buildings shewing above the line of fortifications, and standing out from the hills inland with an air that is both picturesque and stately. The visitor wishing to properly appreciate the natural beauties of the bay should make the ascent of Mount Ancon (540 feet), from which a truly charming bird's-eye view is obtainable; taking in the City, the Islands in the Bay, the long line of Coast on both sides of the Gulf, the inland country, with the chain of the Cordilleras, as well as what exists of the Canal.

The Canal Works may still be considered the principal attraction on the Isthmus. To arrive at a correct appreciation of the undertaking, the partially completed portions of La Boca on the Panama side and Gatun at the Colon end should be inspected; but a fair idea can be obtained by a journey over the railroad—the line running parallel with the intended Canal for a considerable part of the route. It may be mentioned that the Canal was commenced in 1881, was to be $46\frac{1}{2}$ miles long, 124 feet wide at waterline, and 72 feet at bottom, with a depth of 28 feet. When the works ceased in March, 1889, $48\frac{1}{2}$ million cubic feet had been removed, about half of the total excavations ; and to do this £48,000,000 had been spent.

The 1st class fare from Panama to Colon is $10 American gold, or £2 1/8. The distance is 45 miles, and the time occupied on the journey about an hour-and-a-quarter.

The offices of The Pacific Steam Navigation Company are in the Central Square, close to the Cathedral. Steamers arrive from and leave for the South every week.

BUENAVENTURA, situated at the mouth of the Cauca valley, and 355 miles south of Panama, is one of the chief ports of Colombia, being on the principal route to the Capital from the Pacific. It has a population of 1,200 and a fair commerce, though the town itself has rather a poor appearance. A railway is in course of construction to Cali, 75 miles distant, but at present it reaches only to Córdoba, 12 miles from Buenaventura. Trains leave the port three times a week for Córdoba, and horses from there to Cali are obtainable at from $12 to $15 each for the journey.

The principal towns of the department are :—

Cali, almost in the centre of the remarkably productive valley of the Cauca, and containing 20,000 to 25,000 inhabitants. It is more important than the surrounding towns, and the only one offering hotel accommodation. There is a small steamer at Cali running on the Cauca River.

Palmira, with 15,000 to 20,000 inhabitants; and

Buga, with 10,000 inhabitants. Very little indeed is known of these towns.

The greater part of Colombia, particularly on the Pacific side, is believed to contain rich and almost inexhaustible gold fields, which, if properly exploited, should give immense wealth to the country. At present some of these are being worked in the vicinity of Buenaventura, though only on a very limited scale. In addition to gold ore, the department exports Cocoa, Coffee, Tobacco and India-rubber.

Paper money is the only circulating medium here, the paper dollar being worth about 25d.

Bogotá, the capital of Colombia, has a population of 100,000. It is a fine city, built on an elevated plain some 9000 feet above the sea level, and possesses a delightful climate; it contains many buildings worthy of note, and the natural beauties of the surrounding country are remarkable. Its commerce *via* Buenaventura is not extensive, owing to the limited means of inland communication. The journey from Cali is made on mule back, but the roads are rugged and difficult, the highest pass being about 8000 feet.

The intermediate coasting steamers of The Pacific Steam Navigation Company (Panama-Guayaquil Line) call at Buenaventura, each way, once a fortnight. The Telegraph Cable Company has a station at the port with a land line on to Bogotá.

TUMACO.—A port of Colombia about 40 miles north of the boundary line with Ecuador, and 400 miles south of Panama, with a population of 1,500. The principal exports are gold dust, rubber, ivory nuts, cocoa, coffee, and lumber.

There is no railway at Tumaco, communication with the interior being carried on by horses or mules. Two small river steamers ply between Tumaco and Barbacoas, a town of 4,000 inhabitants, distant two days journey, and the centre of the gold mining district. Fare $15 currency. From Barbacoas there is a mule road passing through Tuquerros (population 7,000) and Thiales (population 5,000) to Pasto (population 19,000), the principal town of the interior, and distant five days journey from Barbacoas. Hotel accommodation is scarce, and not to be relied upon.

This port is served by the Pacific Company's intermediate steamers calling once a week.

CHAPTER VI.

ECUADOR.

ESMERALDAS is the most northern port of Ecuador. It is picturesquely situated close to the mouth of the Esmeraldas River, and bordered by a well watered and richly fertile country. The town has some 4,000 inhabitants; and exports largely tobacco, coffee, cocoa, rubber, cocoanut oil, balsams, and sarsaparilla, as well as gold dust, which is supposed to exist in considerable quantities in the neighbouring districts of Cachavi, Santiago and Cayapas. A company has recently been formed in the United States for the exploitation of these deposits on an extensive scale. In the vicinity several emerald mines were formerly worked, and from these the town took its name; they have, however, long since been abandoned or are worked only on a reduced scale.

This port is served by the intermediate coasting steamers.

BAHIA, 137 miles south of Esmeraldas, is situated at the mouth of the Caracas River. The port is difficult of access, but is largely visited by small sailing vessels on account of its extensive cocoa exportation, this forming the principal industry of the surrounding country. A railway from Bahia to Quito is in project, which, if built, will greatly enhance the importance of the town; in the meantime a good road is being made.

The intermediate steamers call here once a fortnight.

MANTA, 31 miles south of Bahia, is chiefly devoted to trade in straw plait (hats, hammocks, &c.) manufactured in the neighbouring inland towns; it also exports ivory nuts, rubber, cocoanut oil, vanilla, &c. This part of the coast formerly possessed important pearl fisheries, but they are now almost abandoned. The principal towns in the vicinity are Portoviejo, the capital of the province, 40 miles distant; Montecristi, 9 miles distant, Jipijapa and Santa Ana, almost entirely occupied in the straw plait industry.

Six miles north of Montecristi, at Cerro de Hoja, is a curious Indian relic, consisting of a table and a number of carved chairs hewn from solid blocks of stone and placed in a circle on the summit of a flat-topped hill. The table is said to weigh about 40 tons. This is supposed to have been the place of council for the dignitaries of the Cara tribe of Indians, which in bygone days held sway over these regions.

The Pacific Steam Navigation Company's intermediate steamers call at this port once a month each way.

BALLENITA, at the entrance to the Gulf of Guayaquil, is the sea port for the town of Santa Elena, some two miles inland. There are various salt mines in the vicinity, and the export of this article forms the principal trade of the port. The straw plait industry is carried on in the neighbourhood, and large quantities of straw for the making of hats, &c., are exported along the coast.

The Telegraph Cable Company have a station here, this being the junction for their Guayaquil branch line. The steamers call once a month.

GUAYAQUIL, the principal port of Ecuador, is one of the most important cities of this part of the Pacific Coast. It is situated on the left bank of the Guayas River,

some 40 miles from the mouth, at the foot of three remarkable hills known as the Cerros de la Cruz. The port is

2¼ miles long, with a fine stretch of quays extending for over 1½ miles; and from the river has an imposing appearance, especially at night when the town is lit up. The houses are of wood and cane—large, commodious and brightly decorated.

Guayaquil boasts of a cathedral, several churches, two banks, a theatre, several hotels, a racecourse, and a small shipyard; also sea baths. The latter, about a mile and a half to the back of the town, are supplied from the sea by a natural canal running parallel with the river: a tramway connects the baths with the city.

Guayaquil, being the only outlet for the populous and important provinces of the interior, has a flourishing commerce, exporting cocoa, coffee, sugar, bark, hides and fruit to the value of a million sterling annually. The population is about 45,000.

The Guayas River is the largest watercourse on the coast, and is navigable for a distance of 200 miles. A number of steamers are employed in local traffic, giving communication, by means of the various tributaries, to a vast tract of most fertile country. Off the town the river is over a mile wide, and is rapid and muddy from its mouth to within sight of Guayaquil, the banks being lined with dense Mangrove swamps, but higher up well-cultivated plantations of cocoa, coffee and tropical fruits are to be met with.

There are two routes from Guayaquil to Quito (the capital) one by river to Bodegas 60 miles, thence by mule road through Guaranda, Ambato and Latacunga (population 15,000), a journey of about five days; the other by the railroad in course of construction, at present reaching from Duran (in front of Guayaquil) to Chimbo, a distance of 52 miles, and passing through the towns of Yaguachi, Milagro and Naranjito; thence by mule road through the towns of Sibambe, Alausi, Riobamba (an important town, of 18,000 inhabitants) to Ambato, where it joins the road, already referred to, from Bodegas. The first of these reaches an altitude of 15,000 feet, passing by the side of the famous Chimborazo (21,424 feet) and near to the volcanoes Cotopaxi (18,880 feet) and Tunguragua (16,800 feet).

The cost for the entire journey from Guayaquil to Quito would be about £20; the hotel expenses *en route* being from $2 to $3 per day. Mules are readily obtainable at Bodegas or Chimbo.

Guayaquil is called at by the through Mail steamers once a week each way, is the terminus of the intermediate coast service from Panama, and has sailings fortnightly for the majority of the Ecuadorian and Colombian minor ports. The Telegraph Cable also touches there.

QUITO, the capital of the Republic, is a city of some merit, situated in a ravine at the foot of the volcano

Pichincha (16,500 feet), and at an altitude of 9,543 feet above the sea level, the population being about 70,000. It possesses several handsome squares, in one of which is the cathedral, town hall, palaces of the president and archbishop, and a fine bronze fountain. Among the other buildings of note are several churches and convents, the university, hospital, &c.; there is also liberal hotel accommodation in the city. From Quito eleven snow-capped peaks are visible; among which are Cayambi (19,600 feet), Antisana (19,137 feet), and Sancholagua (17,500 feet).

The principal towns readily accessible from Guayaquil are:—**Bodegas**, with extensive coffee and cocoa estates; **Daule**, devoted to the cultivation of sugar and fruit; **Santa Rosa** (in the Gulf of Guayaquil); **Machala, Balao,** and **Naranjal**—the latter being the port for **Cuenca** (population 30,000)—one of the largest towns of the Republic. In the vicinity of Cuenca are various productive mines of gold, silver and quicksilver; and the locality is rich in specimens of Inca architecture.

The island of Puná, at the mouth of the Guayas River, is the seaside resort of the people of Guayaquil during the rainy season; at other times it is sparsely inhabited, though under the Inca rule it was a populous and important place. It is some 29 miles long by 13 wide, and is the largest of the various islands in the Gulf.

Some 600 miles off the coast, and extending 90 miles on each side of the Equator, are the **Galápagos Islands,** so named from the quantity of turtle caught there—formerly the principal production. The islands are now but thinly populated, and serve only as a station for the whalers cruising about the fishing grounds off the Ecuadorian Coast. The group is of volcanic origin, and is said to have over 2000 craters. Albemarle, the largest island, is 72 miles long, reaching an altitude of 4700 feet in some parts.

The current coin in Ecuador is the Sucre, value about 24*d*.

CHAPTER VII.

PERU.

TUMBES is a small town of 1800 inhabitants, on the Tumbes River, and situated on the boundary line between Peru and Ecuador. It has in the neighbourhood some extensive petroleum deposits, which are now being rapidly developed. At Zorritos, close by, an important refinery has been successfully worked for many years past.

It was near to Tumbes that Pizarro first landed, at a spot known as Comendador Creek, 25 miles south. Tumbes was then a flourishing town, and the ruins of a once-famous temple are still to be seen in the vicinity.

PAYTA (population about 2000) is 120 miles south

of Tumbes, and in point of commerce is the third largest port of Peru. It possesses an hotel, a theatre, churches, &c.; and there is a railway to Piura, the capital of the department, some 60 miles (by rail) inland.

Piura is the most important town in the north, and is the centre of the cotton-growing industry of Peru. It has some 8,000 inhabitants, a branch of the Bank of Callao, Chamber of Commerce, and other public buildings, and possesses a very dry and salubrious climate; on this latter account it is much visited by persons suffering from rheumatism and similar ailments, the method of cure resorted to there having proved very beneficial. There are several very extensive cotton estates traversed by the railway, which, to those interested in cotton culture, would well repay a visit. Trains run daily.

There is also an extension of the line from Piura to **Catacaos**—6 miles distant, and one of the most important centres of the straw hat industry.

To the north of Payta and 55 miles distant, is the small port of **Talara**, remarkable for the extensive petroleum deposits in its vicinity. Several large and important refineries and pumping stations have during the last few years been established in the immediate neighbourhood, and it is believed that the industry is capable of very great development. Special tank steamers are already employed distributing the oil along the coast.

The through steamers of the Pacific Company from and to Panama call at Payta, and the Telegraph Cable Company has also a station there.

PIMENTEL is 152 miles south of Payta. It has a railway serving the inland towns of Chiclayo and Lambayeque, ten and nine miles distant respectively. There is considerable rivalry existing between Pimentel and Eten (the next port), the railways from both towns running through the same districts.

About 50 miles out from the port of Pimentel are the **Islands of Lobos de Afuera,** well known for their extensive guano deposits, and now in the possession of Chile.

Pimentel is the northern terminus of the Pacific Steam Navigation Company's fortnightly intermediate Chilian and Peruvian Coast Line.

ETEN.—This port is situated 9 miles south of Pimentel and 166 miles (direct) from Payta. It has a fine iron pier 2,000 feet long, the railway running out to the pierhead; but the roadstead is exposed, and has a very heavy surf. The valley inside of Eten is well populated and richly fertile, producing sugar, rice, tobacco, &c., in considerable quantities. There is a railway (broad gauge) from Eten to **Pátapo** (30 miles), passing most of the principal towns and estates.

The village of Eten, three miles from the port, is one of the principal centres of the straw plait industry. The hats (Panama straw), cigar cases, &c., made here are much esteemed for their fineness of texture and excellent workmanship, and command very high prices.

The towns of **Chiclayo** (population 13,000), 12 miles from Eten, **Lambayeque** (population 6,250), capital of the province and 29 miles distant, and **Ferreñafe**, 29 miles from Eten, are important commercial centres; in the vicinity are the estates of Cayaltí, Pátapo, Pucalá, Almendral, Tuman, and Pomalca, which produce together some 8,000 tons of sugar and 2,000 tons of rice annually, the total production of rice for the Department being about 10,000 tons per year.

Near to Pucalá are the ruins of a notable Inca fortress.

Eten is served by the through Panama-Callao steamers, and also by the intermediate Coast Line. There is a land telegraph line communicating with Callao.

PACASMAYO is 34 miles south of Eten; population 2,000. There is a fair commercial movement considering the size of the town. The port is good, and possesses a fine pier, 1,000 yards long. The chief exports are sugar, rice and cattle, products of the fertile regions in the vicinity.

There is a railway from Pacasmayo connecting the port with the principal towns of the interior. Trains run to **Guadalupe** daily, and to the Sierra every Monday, upon the following itinerary:

San Pedro	... distance 5 miles.		
Calasnique Junction	... 10 "		
San José ... distance 11 miles	Tecape	... distance 12 miles
Chafan " 15 "	Tolon... " 25 "
Talambo " 20 "	Monte Grande " 33 "
Chepen " 22 "	Tembladera " 30 "
Guadalupe " 27 "	Yonan " 40 "

The principal towns of the interior are:—

Cajamarca, capital of the department of that name, built at the foot of Mount Cumbe (16,000 feet), with a population of 15,000. Cajamarca figures largely in the history of the Conquest, and it was here that Atahualpa was captured by Pizarro and held prisoner.

San Pedro de Lloc, a small town of some 5,000 inhabitants. A tramway unites the town with the railway station, a mile and a-quarter distant.

Chepen, population about 5,000; a centre of commerce with the interior. Near here is the extensive sugar estate of Lurifico.

Guadalupe, population 4,000. An agricultural fair of considerable importance is held here annually, at the commencement of December. The town is also surrounded by several estates of importance.

Pacasmayo is also called at by the through Panama-Callao steamers, as well as by the intermediate Coast boats.

SALAVERRY, 66 miles from Pacasmayo and 256 miles from Callao, is an active commercial seaport, with a population of about 1500. The principal exports are sugar, rice and alcohol, from the neighbouring valleys of Chicama and Chimu; also moderate quantities of metals.

It is connected by rail with the town of Trujillo, as well as with various other places of importance in the interior, the following being the principal stations:—

Trujillo	distance	12 miles
Chicama	"	30 "
Mocollope	"	33 "
Chocope	"	36 "
Tanque	"	41 "
Facalá	"	44 "
Ascope	"	47 "

Trujillo, the Capital of the Department, is one of the most important commercial places of the North. It is a well-built city, with a population of 10,000; is a Bishop's See, and possesses a branch of the Bank of Callao, Chamber of Commerce, Cathedral, and several other buildings of note.

This was one of the first towns founded by Pizarro; and the visitor will therefore find much to interest him from an historical point of view. Some two miles distant are the ruins of an ancient city called Chan Chan, founded by the Chimu tribe of Indians, and which gives evidence of an advanced state of civilization in its inhabitants. There are also, near by, the remains of an Indian Temple to the Sun.

The towns of note inland are:—**Chicama, Chocope** and **Ascope**, the latter being the terminus of the railway, and carrying on a fair trade with the interior. All of these towns are, however, chiefly devoted to Agriculture, and in the vicinity there are some extensive sugar estates, such as:—

Laredo	6 miles from Trujillo.	
Galindo	12 " " "	
Chiquitoy	between Salaverry and Huanchaco.	
Casa Grande	near Tanque.	
Facalá	" Ascope.	
Sausal	" "	
Cartavio	" Trujillo.	

Salaverry is served by the through Panama-Callao steamers, and by the intermediate Coast line; the steamers of the latter also sometimes call at Huanchaco, a small port 13 miles to the North, and dependent upon Salaverry Custom House.

SALAVERRY to CALLAO.—The minor ports from Salaverry to Callao are served by The Pacific Steam Navigation Company's Coast line, running fortnightly between Callao and Pimentel.

The principal of these ports are—

Chimbote, a small town 61 miles to the South of Salaverry, situated in an extensive and well-sheltered Bay, considered by many the finest on the Coast. Inland of the town is a very fertile valley enclosing various extensive sugar estates, such as:—

Puente (or Palo Seco)	9	miles from Chimbote.
Rinconada	14	,, ,, ,,
Viazos	20	,, ,, ,,
Monnt Hermoso	21	,, ,, ,,
Suchiman	25	,, ,, ,,

These are passed by the railway which at present runs from Chimbote to Suchiman only, but which it is the intention to carry on to the southern extremity of the valley of Huaylas.

There are in the interior various silver mines of importance being worked.

Samanco and **Casma** are small seaport towns, shipping metals from the mining districts in the interior, and also small quantities of sugar.

Huarmey, 43 miles south of Casma. The Ticapampa Mining Co. have extensive silver producing establishments inland from this port.

Supe and Huacho, 90 and 70 miles from Callao respectively, export sugar and cotton from some fairly important estates in the vicinity, as well as metals from the interior. Inside of Huacho is a very fertile valley, from which Lima and Callao draw large supplies of agricultural produce and fruit.

At all of the above ports there is a land telegraph line communicating with Callao and Lima.

CALLAO, the principal port of Peru, has a good harbour, a very fine dock and breakwater. The hotel

accommodation is fair. The population now about 20,000, has fallen off considerably since the war with Chile.

At La Punta, about two miles to the south of Callao,

there are several good hotels and excellent bathing. This place being at the extremity of the neck of land separating Callao Bay from Chorrillos Bay, and exposed to the sea breezes from the south and north, enjoys a bracing and healthy climate, and is much esteemed by invalids on this account. There is a railroad between La Punta and Callao. The hotel rates are moderate, from $2 to $3 per day.

The Pacific Steam Navigation Company have an Office and extensive Factories and Depôts at Callao.

LIMA, the capital, is about eight miles inland from Callao, and is connected therewith by two railways, that of the English Railway Co. and the Ferro-Carril Central del Peru.

Lima is the second largest city of the South Pacific, and possesses many fine squares and churches, a prettily arranged park, a public library and other buildings, which merit a visit. The city is built on the banks of the river Rimac, some 500 feet above the sea level, and possesses a very equable and agreeable climate. It has a population, according to the last census (1891), of 103,956.

Lima will, however, perhaps be found of still greater interest from an historical point of view; as, being the first and last of the Spanish Colonies on this coast, it still retains many indications of the conquest and colonisation. The cathedral is a fine and extensive building, and, like most of the churches in Lima, dates from the days of the Spaniards; the architecture in all being of the simple and heavy style common to that period. The remains of Pizarro, founder of Lima, which were formerly preserved in the cathedral, have now been removed to a specially erected chapel in the presidential palace. There are still a few private houses dating from the colonisation in existence, and some of these are remarkable for the richness of the carving, &c., of the façades. In the summer the river is of considerable proportions, but in the winter it is only an insignificant mountain stream; it is, however, crossed by three fine bridges, one of stone built by the Spaniards, and the others of iron, of recent structure and considerable merit.

The city is covered by a very complete system of tramways, and the principal streets are lighted by electricity. Hotels are numerous and good, and the tariffs moderate.

In the vicinity of Lima, and connected therewith by direct lines of rail, are the seaside resorts of Ancon, Magdalena, Miraflores, Barranco and Chorrillos, much frequented during the summer by the people of Lima and Callao.

The only means of communication between Lima and the mountain regions is by the Oroya Railroad (Ferro-Carril Central del Peru). This railroad is justly considered one of the most prominent features of interest on the coast, not only as being a fine specimen of modern engineering, but also for the grandeur and originality of the scenery brought before the traveller. Some of the tunnelling and bridge work is very remarkable and will well repay inspection, especially the second Verrugas Bridge, which has been recently built to supply the place of a former structure destroyed by floods in 1888. It is on the cantilever principle, with one centre span 235 feet long, in the clear, and two shore spans of 140 feet each; and is 257 feet from the bottom of the ravine it crosses. The grade for the line is 4 per cent.

A general idea of the road may be gathered from the following table of altitudes, &c. :—

Distance. English Miles.	Stations.	Elevation above sea level. English feet.	Fares.
—	Callao, Terminus	8.7	—
4.3	La Legua		
7.7	Lima, Monserrate Station	499.9	
8.1	Lima, La Palma Station	—	
8.4	Lima, Desamparados Station		
9.0	Lima, Viterbo Station		.40
18.0	Santa Clara Station	1,311.7	.90c
33.2	Chosica Station	2,800.6	$1.60
40.3	Puruay Bridge	—	—
40.8	Corcona Bridge		

Distance. English Miles.	STATIONS.	Elevation above sea level. English feet.	Fares.
45.0	Cocachacra Estate	4,622.6	
47.1	St. Bartolome Station and Viaduct	4,959.4	$2.95
51.0	Verrugas Bridge	5,839.4	
52.8	Cuesta Blanca Tunnel	6,001.1	
55.0	Surco Station	6,660.0	$3.80
61.1	Challapa Bridge	7,594.1	
63.6	Matucana Station	7,788.8	$4.80
65.5	Quebrada Negra Bridge	8,054.1	
68.8	Tambo de Viso Bridge	8,706.5	
73.0	Chaupichaca Bridge	9,472.6	
74.9	Tamboraque Viaduct	9,826.9	
76.3	Aruri Viaduct	10,094.5	
78.5	San Mateo Station	10,534.1	$6.00
80.4	Infiernillo Bridge	10,919.9	
81.0	Charray Double Viaduct	11,033.1	
82.5	Anchi Bridge	11,306.4	
84.2	Copa Bridge	11,638.8	
87.2	Chicla Station, New Lower Viaduct	12,215.5	$6.80
90.0	Chicla Upper Viaduct	12,607.1	
95.0	Casapalca Double Viaduct	13,840.0	—
105.0	Galera Pass, Tunnel 2,032 yards long, highest point of the line	15,665.0	
—	Mount Meiggs Peak, 17,575 feet high	17,575.1	
120.1	Vauli Station	13,420.8	
136.5	Oroya	12,178.7	

At present, however, the line extends only as far as Casapalca; though the continuation to the village of Oroya, on the other side of the Cordilleras, and on the river of that name, is well in hand. Government engineers are now engaged in laying out a new and intended important town in the vicinity of the present village of Oroya.

There are fairly good hotels at Chosica, Matucana and Chicla.

Though the coast of Peru is, for the most part, arid and unattractive, the interior is richly luxuriant and fertile, yielding in abundance many descriptions of produce, as well as barks and medicinal herbs of much esteem. In fact, the mineral and vegetable products of the country would be a source of immense wealth, were it not for the very indifferent means of communication between the interior and the coast, and the consequent scanty population; thousands of square miles of land being as yet totally unexplored. The towns on the east of the Cordilleras are, with but few exceptions, little more than villages, inhabited mostly by Indians and half-breeds. Those worthy of note are:—

Cerro de Pasco, 12,000 inhabitants, one of the richest mining districts in the country. It is situated at an altitude of 16,500 feet, and about 100 miles north of Oroya. A line of rail connecting this town with Oroya is shortly to be built.

Tarma, a thriving commercial town some 15 miles to the east of Oroya. It has a population of about 9,000, and is well spoken of on account of its dry and temperate climate.

Jauja, at an altitude of 11,150 feet, is the chief resort of consumptives and persons suffering from bronchial affections, its climate being peculiarly beneficial in such cases. Apart from its high standing as a health resort, Jauja is not a town of much importance, though under the Inca rule it was a flourishing and populous city. The population of the town and its suburbs is said to be 21,000. It is situated about 30 miles to the south of Tarma and 50 miles south of Oroya.

There are also the towns of **Concepcion** and **Huancayo** to the south, and **Chanchamayo** to the east of Tarma, and distant about two days' mule ride; and **Huanuco** a similar distance to the north of Cerro de Pasco.

Under the Contract with the Bond-holders, the following extensions of the Oroya Railroad are to be made :—

> Oroya to Tarma, Concepcion and Huancayo.
> Oroya to Cerro de Pasco.
> Cerro de Pasco to Mairo (near to the German Colony of Pozuzo on the banks of the River Pozuzo, and some 200 miles inland from Oroya).
> Tarma to the River Ucayali (the principal navigable tributary of the Amazon).

The latter is an undertaking of considerable importance, as it will establish, by rail and river, direct communication across the centre of the Continent between the Pacific and Atlantic Oceans, and will also accelerate the much needed colonization of the wealthiest regions of Peru.

The Pacific Steam Navigation Company's steamers leave Callao both for the south and north at frequent intervals, itineraries and tariffs being obtainable at any of the Company's Agencies.

The current coin in Peru is the silver "sol," worth from 34d to 37d, according to the rate of exchange.

There is cable communication from Callao with all parts of the world. Postage for letters, via Panama, is 11 cents per 15 grammes, and 10 cents for the same weight via the Straits of Magellan.

CERRO AZUL, 72 miles south of Callao, is a surf port, dependent upon the Callao Custom House. It exports fair quantities of sugar from the adjacent valley of Cañete. The chief town of the district, **Cañete,** is about five miles inland.

The Pacific Company's steamers call at Cerro Azul once a fortnight each way.

TAMBO DE MORA is a minor port, 105 miles south of Callao, and 14 miles north of Pisco; chiefly occupied in the export of wine, cotton, sugar and agricultural produce, from the rich valley of Chincha, the estimated produce of which is 224,000 gallons of aguardiente (brandy), 12,500 gallons wine, 1,200 barrels rum and 15,000 quintals of cotton per year. The town of **Chincha** is situated six miles from the port of Tambo de Mora.

The steamers call here twice a week each way.

PISCO, 116 miles south of Callao, serves as the outlet for a rich and fertile valley covering an extensive area. Though chiefly devoted to the culture of the vine and cotton, for which its climate is particularly suitable, it exports in large quantities all kinds of agricultural produce. The town of Pisco contains about 4000 inhabitants; it possesses a tramway, and a fine pier 600 yards long; also a railway to Ica, the capital of the department, 46 miles distant.

ICA has a population of 10,000, devoted to wine and cotton production, and commerce with the interior. It is a neatly built and well-situated town; and in the immediate vicinity are several small medicinal lakes, highly recommended for diseases of the skin and stomach, and for rheumatism. The province of Ica is said to produce 700,000 gallons wine, 90,000 gallons spirits, and 40,000 quintals cotton annually.

The principal towns in the interior are:—

Huancavelica, population 9000, 120 miles from Ica. Close to this town is the famous quicksilver mine of Santa Barbara.

Ayacucho, population 10,000, 182 miles from Ica. Remarkable filagree work, and other specimens of the silversmith's art are produced here.

Castrovireyna, some 100 miles from Ica, a mining district of considerable note.

Ica is the highway to all of these places.

Ten miles out from Pisco are the **Chincha Islands**, once famous for their guano deposits, from which Peru obtained an immense revenue.

Steamers call at Pisco twice a week in both directions. There is a land telegraph line from Lima to Pisco and Ica.

LOMAS, 152 miles from Pisco and 201 miles from Mollendo.

CHALA, 200 miles from Pisco and 159 miles from Mollendo.

Both of these places are but of minor importance, the staple productions of the surrounding country being cattle, which are shipped along the Coast in large quantities, minerals, wool and cotton. There are various silver and copper mines being worked in the interior.

The only town of consideration in the neighbourhood is Coracora.

About 30 miles to the north-east of Chala is the volcano Achataihua, 13,800 feet high.

Steamers call at Lomas and Chala, alternately, once a week each way.

MOLLENDO, the second port of the Republic, is a town of 5000 inhabitants. It possesses two hotels, and is of considerable importance commercially; as, being the port for

Arequipa, Cuzco, &c., as well as for the interior towns of
Bolivia, it ships large quantities of alpaca and sheep's wool,
skins, coca leaves, bark, silver, tin and copper ores, to the

MOLLENDO.

value of about £400,000 annually. It is the western
terminus of the railway to Santa Rosa (Cuzco), Puno and
La Paz (Bolivia).

AREQUIPA, the capital of the department, is a city
of about 30,000 inhabitants, built at the foot of the extinct
volcano Misti (18,650 feet high), and at an altitude of 7550
feet above the sea level. It is an important commercial
city, and not without interest to the visitor; is well built
(the houses being constructed generally of blocks of lava);
has a cathedral, a bank, chamber of commerce, theatre, and
some good hotels, as well as a club. There are several
thermal baths in the immediate neighbourhood, and on
account of its altitude the town enjoys a pleasant and
healthy climate.

Between Arequipa and Puno various silver mines are being profitably worked on a large scale.

From Arequipa the line extends to Puno, a neatly-built city of some 6,600 inhabitants, on the shores of Lake Titicaca. Puno is at present the eastern terminus of the railway into Bolivia, though the line is about to be continued to La Paz direct.

The remarkable Lake Titicaca lies across the boundary line between Peru and Bolivia; it is situated at an altitude of 12,500 feet above the sea level, and has an area of over 5000 square miles. Two fairly commodious steamers ply on the lake regularly in connection with the arrival of the trains at Puno, and convey passengers across to Chililaya (Bolivia), a distance of 90 miles. From Chililaya there is a coach service to La Paz, seven hours distant. The journey from Mollendo to La Paz is made up as follows:—

```
Mollendo to Arequipa ............... 107 miles
Arequipa to Puno .................... 218  "
Puno to Chililaya ................... 90  "
Chililaya to La Paz ................. 7 hours
```

La Paz is now the capital of Bolivia, and almost all the commerce with the interior is carried on through that town. It contains some 26,000 inhabitants, and being situated at a considerable altitude enjoys an agreeable climate, though the surrounding country is barren and poor. There are five fairly good hotels in La Paz.

Sucre, the former capital, is some 70 miles to the south, and is a fairly extensive city, with a population of about 40,000. Near to Sucre is the town of **Potosi**, renowned for its rich silver mines. These mines are said to be inexhaustible, and it is calculated that, since they were first systematically worked in 1545, they have produced metal to the value of many hundreds of millions sterling. Potosi is said to have once contained as many as 160,000 inhabitants; it has now about 40,000. The town has an altitude of 11,000 feet above the sea level. Mr. F. Suarez, Consul-General of Bolivia, wrote to the *Times* on the 11*th* July, 1895, as follows: " I think it right in the interests of humanity, and especially on behalf of the numerous persons in these islands who suffer so terribly from consumption, to draw attention to the great benefit such sufferers would derive if they would undertake the journey to Bolivia. The air in the regions of 'La Paz,' Sucre, and Oruro is so highly rarefied and dry that it kills the bacilli, the length of time required depending upon the stage the disease has attained; patients in the first or second stage would be completely cured after a short sojourn, but those in the third stage would probably have to remain a few years. No doctors or medicine are required, the air being all that is necessary, although an almost complete abstinence from alcoholic drinks is essential. If persons in the earlier stage of the complaint would go without delay, they would after a few months be able to return completely restored to health. Numerous persons suffering from consumption are annually sent to Italy, &c., where a cure is generally hopeless, whereas, if they would only undertake the longer journey to Bolivia, they would in most cases regain their health."

Cochabamba, capital of the department of the same name, is 270 miles from La Paz; it is about the only other town of any importance in Bolivia. The population is said to be 50,000, mostly Indians. It is situated at an altitude of 8,370 feet above the sea level. Cochabamba is a Bishop's See.

The Cuzco branch of the line is now being extended to Sicuani, within three days' mule ride from Cuzco, and is expected to give a decided impetus to traffic in this direction and to open up the surrounding richly fertile districts. Sicuani is at an altitude of 12,000 feet above the sea level; it is not a large town, but there is one hotel with fair accommodation. The distance thence to Cuzco is 80 miles, but the roads are good, and mules are easily obtainable; the rates are $10 for each passenger mule and $6 each for baggage—each animal carrying about 300 lbs. The fare from Mollendo to Sicuani is $27. Passengers have to remain one night at the junction town Juliaca, where, however, good hotel accommodation is obtainable.

The city of **Cuzco** is supposed to have been founded by Manco Capac, the first Inca, in 1043, and it was taken by Pizarro in 1543. The population is about 18,500. Visitors to this interesting locality will find much to attract their attention, as, being the ancient capital of the Incas, it still possesses many remarkable relics of their empire, particularly the great Temple of the Sun, which furnished such prodigious wealth to the Spanish invaders, the palaces of Manco Capac and his successors, the Inca canal, etc. The ruins of the famous Inca fortress of Saxihuaman attract visitors from all parts of the world. The more modern constructions of note are the cathedral, one of the finest and most remarkable buildings of the kind in the country, the university, museum, cloth factory, and several other buildings. The city is situated at an altitude of 11,000 feet above the sea level.

Cuzco exports large quantities of cocoa, chocolate, coffee, vanilla, coca, indigo, sarsaparilla, quinine and other medicinal barks and herbs, all of which are abundantly produced in the neighbourhood. Considerable quantities of gold are also yearly exported from the Carabaya district in the vicinity; and engineers have been sent out from Europe to survey this with a view to a systematic exploitation of its hidden wealth.

Hotel accommodation in Cuzco is limited, there being only one establishment worth consideration; but visitors not caring to avail themselves of this will find quite a remarkable hospitality in private houses.

Fifteen miles from Cuzco is the valley of Urubamba, the summer resort of the people of Cuzco, 9,000 feet above the sea level. The celebrated ruins of Ollanta and Tambo, ancient fortifications of the Incas, are situated in this valley.

The train service from Mollendo is arranged as follows :—

To BOLIVIA.

Leave	Mollendo	Tuesday, Wednesday, Thursday, Saturday.
„	Arequipa	Wednesday, Sunday.
„	Puno for Chilliaya, steamer	Thursday, Monday.
„	Chililaya, return	Saturday, Tuesday.
„	Puno	Monday, Thursday.
„	Arequipa	Monday, Tuesday, Wednesday, Friday.

To CUZCO.

Leave Arequipa	Sunday.		Leave Santa Rosa	Wednesday.
„ Juliaca	Monday.		„ Puno	Thursday.
Arrive Santa Rosa	Monday.		Arrive Arequipa	Thursday.

The following table of altitudes and distances of the line will be of interest to the visitor :—

Dist'nce English Miles.	STATIONS.	Altitude English Feet.	Dist'nce English Miles.	STATIONS.	Altitude English Feet.
—	Mollendo	6	68	Sumbay	13,618
9¼	Mejia	10	72	Sumbay Bridge	13,413
13½	Ensenada	32	96	Vincocaya	14,360
19	Tambo	1,000	118	Crucero Alto	14,666
25	Posco	1,830	127	Lagunillas	14,250
29½	Cahuintala	2,493	140	Saracocha	13,940
34½	Cachendo	3,250	148	Santa Lucia	13,250
41	Huagri	3,740	155½	Maravillas	13,000
54	La Joya	4,141	168½	Cabanillas	12,750
64½	San Jose	4,850	189	Juliaca	12,550
76]	Vitor	5,350	218	Puno	12,540
84	Quishuarani	6,125		FROM JULIACA.	
94½	Uchumayo	6,450	14	Calapuja	12,565
100	Tiabaya	6,750	21	Nicacio	12,652
105	Tingo	7,275	25	Laro	12,727
107	Arequipa	7,550	35	Pucara	12,738
	FROM AREQUIPA.		42	Tirapata	12,731
18	Yura	8,450	58	Ayaviri	12,807
26	Aguas Calientes	9,500	60	Chuquibambilla	12,832
44	Puente de Arrieros	12,300	82	Santa Rosa	13,100
58½	Canaguas	13,380		Sicuani	12,000

Some notable peaks are visible on the way, such as:

Urbinas (volcano)	16,000 feet	About 50 miles South of Arequipa.
Charchani	19,002 "	To the North of the Misti.
Pichupichu	17,800 "	To the East of the Misti.
Coropuna	22,000 "	Visible from P. de Arrieros Station.
Apucuararani	17,500 "	Close to Santa Rosa.
Vilcanota	17,550 "	Between Santa Rosa and Sicuani.
Sorata	21,286 "	East shore of Lake Titicaca.
Illimani	21,148 "	South-East of La Paz.

The Lakes of Saracocha and Cachipascana are also in close proximity to the line, at an altitude of 13,500 feet above the sea level; but the bordering country all along the route will be found to be barren and rugged in the extreme, presenting a most inhospitable aspect.

The regular through steamers call at Mollendo, north-bound, every Sunday and Wednesday; going south, calls are made every Tuesday and Saturday. There is a telegraph cable station there, and land lines communicate with Arequipa, Cuzco and La Paz.

ILO is a minor port about half way between Mollendo and Arica. Its chief trade is the export of wines, spirits and olives, for which the surrounding districts have a high reputation.

MOQUEGUA, the capital of the province of the same name, is about 55 miles inland. A railway formerly existed to Ilo, but this was destroyed during the war with Chile, and has not since been rebuilt. The town has about 3500 inhabitants.

CHAPTER VIII.

CHILE.

ARICA is at present the northernmost port held by Chile, the two provinces of Tacna and Arica having been taken possession of by that country at the close of the late war with Peru.

The town is small (population about 3000), clean and regularly built; it possesses a magnificent bay with a good iron pier, and carries on an active commerce with the interior, exporting wool, hides and metals in considerable quantities. It is almost enclosed by sand hills, and is built at the foot of a steep and

MORRO DE ARICA.

remarkable mount, some 500 feet high, called the Morro, which, during the late war, was the scene of a fierce and memorable struggle between the contending parties.

TACNA, the capital, some 80 miles distant, is separated from Arica by a stretch of desert, where at times the mirage is to be seen to perfection: there is, however, railway communication between the two towns, trains running daily each way. It has a population of about 8000, and though surrounded for the most part by sandy hills and plains, is one of the most pleasing and neatly arranged of the Coast towns. The hotel accommodation is ample and good.

Tacna is almost entirely occupied in traffic with

Bolivia; at present, however, the means of communication is by mule tracks, but there is a telegraph line, and a railway is in project. There is a road to Oruro, the Southern province of Bolivia, and another to La Paz, a distance of 240 miles—about 8 days' ride.

The snow-capped peak of Tacora (15,000 feet) is visible from Tacna, and in the vicinity of the routes to La Paz and Oruro are the Volcano Gualatieri (22,500 feet), and the peaks Parinacoto (22,600 feet), Pomarape (22,450 feet), Sahama (22,350 feet), Kenuta (19,200 feet), Pettagua (17,700 feet), Chipicani (16,000 feet), and Cancana (15,500 feet).

There is Telephonic communication between Arica and Tacna, and the Telegraph Cable Company also has a station at the port. Steamers from the North call at Arica every Sunday and Wednesday, and from the South on Tuesdays and Saturdays.

PISAGUA is situated 70 miles South of Arica, and is a port of some consideration on account of its proximity to the Nitrate fields. It is built on the water's edge at the foot of a semi-circular range of hills, 1200 feet high, entirely shutting it in on the land side. The town itself does not call for any special mention, but the climate is salubrious. The population is about 5000.

The railway from Pisagua to the Nitrate fields is an important feature of the port; it is cut into the sides of the hills at the back of the town, and ascends by a series of zigzags, till it reaches a stretch of table-land or pampa at the top, this it crosses to where a second range, at a distance of some 16 miles from the Coast, rises to a height of 3600 feet, capped by another pampa of vast proportions reaching to the foot of the main chain of the Andes, and here are situated the principal Nitrate establishments. Trains for the Pampa leave Pisagua three times a week, returning on alternate days, and the line is in direct communication with Iquique. There are hotels at some of the Stations, but visitors can almost count upon ample hospitality at any of the Nitrate establishments, as well as facilities for inspecting the works, &c.

The through steamers call at Pisagua from the north every Sunday and Wednesday, and from the south every Tuesday and Saturday. There is also cable communication via Iquique.

IQUIQUE.—This port, well known for its nitrate trade, is built on a sandy plain entirely shut in landwards by a semi-circular range of hills some 2000 feet high. It is a well built city for a coast town ; the streets are wide, airy and regular ; the houses, built of timber for the most part, and arranged in rectangular blocks, are gaily coloured ; and the town altogether presents a lively appearance. It has the customary "plaza" or central square adorned with a monument to the naval hero Arthur Prat; also a cathedral and various churches, several banks, a public library,

PLAZA DE IQUIQUE

numerous well-found hotels, three clubs, the Government Houses, a High Court of Appeal, theatre, racecourse, cricket ground, tramways, electric light, telephones, and in fact almost every convenience to be found in a modern European town. The population is about 20,000.

The principal business of Iquique is the shipment of nitrate of soda and iodine sent down from the Pampas, but there are also a number of wealthy gold and silver mines in the locality, particularly Huantajaya, Descubridora, Constantia, Paquanta, Colorada; all notable for their rich productions.

Communication with the nitrate fields is carried on

by means of a broad gauge railway (4 ft. 8½ in.), from the port, traversing the Pampa and terminating at the Lagunas, a distance of 239¼ miles. This passes through the principal nitrate producing districts, serving the large number of "Oficinas" in the vicinity by means of a series of short branches and offshoots. A journey over this road will be found most instructive to those interested in this class of industry, or who may wish to obtain a fair idea of the peculiarities of life and work on the Pampa; as the majority

of the principal establishments are situated in close proximity to the line. Apart from the factories and the sparse habitations of the native labourers, the Pampa is a barren desert devoid of either life or vegetation, in fact more resembling the bed of a vast inland sea than anything else. Darwin decribes it as follows :—" The appearance of the country was remarkable from being covered with a thick crust of common salt and of a stratified saliferous alluvium, which seems to have been deposited as the land rose slowly above the sea. The appearance of this superficial mass very closely resembled that of a country after snow, before the last dirty patches are thawed." At the Central Station (3220 feet above the sea level) the Trunk Line from Iquique joins that from Pisagua and thence strikes east and south, with various minor branches to the neighbouring " Oficinas."

The export of nitrate during 1894 from the four ports of Tarapaca, between Iquique and Pisagua inclusive, was 890,816 tons, the principal producing establishments being :—

" Rosario de Huara," " Ramirez " or the Liverpool Nitrate, "San Jorge," "La Palma" and "La Patria," "Agua Santa," " Lagunas," " La Paccha " and " Jaz Pampa," and " Buena Ventura."

There are two Telegraph Cable Stations at Iquique, and land wires serve all the coast towns. Steamers call Southbound on Mondays and Thursdays, and Northbound on same days ; the Intermediate Steamers from Valparaiso also make regular calls at the port.

Twenty miles north of Iquique is the minor port of **Caleta Buena**, serving as port of shipment for the extensive Nitrate establishment of " Agua Santa," which is 21 miles inland. From the top of the hill to the beach, the railway cars are let down by a cable, but from the top of the hill the railway to the interior is a 2 ft. 6 in. narrow gauge line, worked by ordinary locomotives.

Some 10 miles north of Caleta Buena is the small Nitrate port of **Junin**. The " Jaz Pampa " Oficina, as well as others, ships from here

TOCOPILLA, 117 miles south of Iquique, formerly a Bolivian port, was taken possession of by Chile in 1879 It is a sheltered port, and, after Valparaiso, has the finest iron pier (fitted with hydraulic cranes, &c., on the Coast. The principal industry of the place is copper mining, which has, however, somewhat fallen off of late ; nitrate of soda is also a leading article of export.

The Anglo-Chilian and Nitrate Railway runs from the port to Toco, the centre of the nitrate district, 50 miles inland, where there is a large virgin extent of Nitrate grounds, in which the Railway Company is interested. The railway runs up 5000 feet in the first 30 miles, then down 1500 feet to Toco. Near to that town there are also considerable deposits of borax, though up to the present these have not been worked to any extent.

The population of Tocopilla is small; the climate is warm and dry, and is considered very healthy. There is a fairly good hotel in the port, and the steamers call there once a week each way.

COBIJA, a minor port 31 miles South of Tocopilla, is small and sparsely populated, and its existence is solely dependent upon the mining industry of the vicinity. It exports good quantities of ores; copper, tin and some silver.

The steamers call at Cobija once a week each way.

ANTOFAGASTA is a rising port situated on the border of the great desert of Atacama, 232 miles south of

Iquique. It was formerly the chief port of Bolivia, but at the termination of the late war was ceded to Chile. The population now numbers about 9,000, and is on the increase, and as the rich mineral districts of the interior are being rapidly opened up, and the resources of the country developed, a good future may be expected for the port. At present there are several smelting establishments in full operation, and the quantity of metals—gold, silver, and copper—as well as of nitrate of soda and borate of lime, exported is very considerable; in fact, the deposit of borate near Ascotan, which is now being actively worked, is one of the most extensive known, and the calcining of this material forms an important industry of the town.

Antofagasta is the port for the famous silver mines of Huanchaca, as well as for the southern departments of Bolivia, and a narrow gauge (2 ft. 6 in.) railway runs from the port to Oruro, a distance of 570 miles. To those interested in mining operations, or who may wish to obtain a good idea of the country, this journey will be particularly attractive, as the visitor will find the various industries displayed to him in a large number of their different phases. For instance, he will traverse the nitrate fields, pass the silver mines of Caracoles, Inca, Loa, San Cristobal, Potosi, Huanchaca, and Colquechaca; the copper mines of Lomas, Bayos, Conchicul, and Aralar; the valley of the Loa, with its interesting mineralogical and archæological remains; the active volcanoes of San Pedro, San Pablo, and Ollagua;

the elevated tableland lakes of Ascotan and Carcot, the sulphur mines and borate deposits of Ascotan, the tin mines of Oruro, and the bismuth mines of Lipez; all of which are served by the line. From Oruro there is a coach service through Sucre and the famous mining district of Colquechaca to La Paz—a four days' journey.

Huanchaca is one of the most renowned and best producing silver districts in the world; its export in 1890 amounting to 5,608,376 ounces of fine silver, in addition to large quantities coined and distributed in Bolivia and the Argentine Republic. It is owned by a Bolivian Company, and the smelting works they are now having erected in Antofagasta promise to be the most extensive and complete establishments of the kind in South America.

There are two comfortable hotels in Antofagasta (pension $4 currency per day), and good accommodation is to be found all along the route; most of the hotels belonging to the railway company. Trains leave Antofagasta for the interior three times a week, returning the following day; and sleeping cars are provided on all. The following is a table of fares and distances on the line:—

Miles.		Fares.	
—	Antofagasta		
51	Cuevitas	$4.00	
80	Salinas	6.00	
106	S. Gorda	7.80	Chilian Currency.
149	Calama	10.80	
187	Conchi	14.00	
225	Ascotan	16.80	
272	Ollagua	19.00	

Miles.		Fares.	
322	Julaca	4.00	Bolivianos at
381	Uyuni Huanchaca	8.00	31d per dollar.
570	Oruro		

Steamers call at Antofagasta, southbound, on Saturdays and Tuesdays; northbound on Sundays and Wednesdays. The telegraph cable touches at the port, and there is also telegraphic communication by land wires with all the Chilian ports.

TALTAL, 131 Miles south of Antofagasta, derives its importance solely from the mining and nitrate industries of the surrounding country. It has a population of 5,000, but, like most of the North Chilian coast towns, is bare of all vegetation, and its water supply has for the greater part of the year to be condensed.

The bay is good, there are two piers, and a considerable number of vessels visit the port. There are in the neighbourhood extensive nitrate and borax deposits, as well as some very productive gold, silver, and copper mines.

The Taltal Railway Company has a line from the port to Cachinal 93 miles long, passing through several nitrate grounds, and close to the Guanaco gold mining district, with various branches running into the principal nitrate "oficinas."

Taltal possesses several smelting establishments with fair output. The hotel accommodation at the port is passable.

There is a land telegraph line connecting the port with the coast; Steamers call there twice a week each way.

CHAÑARAL is a port of 3000 inhabitants on the edge of the Desert of Atacama, 46 miles north of Caldera and 67 miles south of Taltal. It is one of the principal centres of the copper industry in Chile; and has also a large number of gold, silver, nickel, and cobalt mines, as well as nitrate and borax fields, in the vicinity.

The port is connected by two lines of railway with the mining villages and districts of Las Animas and Salado; the former 22, and the latter 24 miles distant. The bay is large and well sheltered, and the climate is cool, dry, and healthy; strong westerly winds prevailing during the day, and cold land breezes at night. There is no vegetation in or near the town, and the drinking water is condensed. Beyond the smelting works and the mines, there is nothing here to interest the visitor. There are two hotels.

Steamers touch at Chañaral in each direction once a week.

CALDERA (108 miles south of Taltal) is the principal port of the province of Atacama, and the outlet for an extensive and wealthy mineral district producing largely gold, silver, and copper in bar and ore. The town is small, but it has a magnificent bay and a fine pier. The population is 2,100.

A railway runs from Caldera to Copiapo, the chief town of the province, whence there are branches to the mining districts of Chañarcillo and San Antonio, distant about 60 miles to the south, as well as to Puquios, 40 miles to the north. From the latter point an extension is in project to Tinogasta on the Argentine side, crossing the Cordilleras at an altitude of 16,000 feet, and then joining the trunk line from Rosario, and passing through some of the most fertile districts of the Argentine Republic.

Copiapo is a neatly-arranged town of 10,000 inhabitants, situated in a fertile valley 50 miles inland of Caldera. It is one of the chief mining centres of Chile, and owns some important smelting establishments and gold mills. The climate is dry and healthy, and both in Caldera and Copiapo there are fair hotels (pension about $2.50 per day). Passable accommodation is also to be found at the various termini of the line.

Trains run daily to Copiapo, and every other day to the interior.

Steamers call at the port, southbound, on Sundays and Thursdays; northbound, on Saturdays and Mondays. The Telegraph Cable Co. has also a station at the port.

CARRIZAL BAJO is a small port 72 miles South of Caldera, the outlet for the productive mineral districts of the interior. It is connected by rail with Carrizal Alto, 23 miles distant, the principal town in the vicinity and formerly a flourishing centre of the copper mining industry. These mines are now, however, almost worked out, and the neighbourhood has, in consequence, fallen off considerably in population and importance. There are also branches of the line to Cerro Blanco Copper Mines, distant 62 miles; to Jarillas Copper Mines, distant 58 miles; and one in course of construction to the Manganese Mines, distant 38 miles. The principal exports are Copper and Manganese ores—from 2,000 to 3,000 tons of the latter being produced monthly.

Trains run daily to the interior, and there is passable hotel accommodation both in Alto and Bajo Carrizal. Steamers call at the port once a week each way.

HUASCO, a small and desolate looking port about half way between Caldera and Coquimbo, is situated at the mouth of the Huasco River, and in a very fertile valley, yielding all kinds of agricultural produce. Excellent wine is produced in the neighbourhood, and the raisins of Huasco are considered by many equal to those of Málaga. The interior is fairly rich in mines of gold, silver, copper, cobalt and manganese; and the port possesses a smelting establishment with a good output. The population is about 1,200.

A railway is in course of construction up the valley to Freirina and Vallenar, the two principal towns inland.

FREIRINA, 13 miles from the port, has a population of 13,000. The locality is rich in gold, copper and manganese.

VALLENAR, 45 miles from Huasco, with a population of 17,000, produces copper, gold, silver and manganese. Near here is the well-known silver mine of Agua Amarga.

Both of these towns are on the River Huasco.

Steamers call at Huasco once a week in both directions.

COQUIMBO is the chief port of an extensive province bearing the same name, and is situated in a fine and well-sheltered bay 200 miles North of Valparaiso. It is a Naval Station of the British Fleet on the Pacific Coast, and, on account of the fine situation of the harbour, is frequently visited by war vessels. The town has some 6,000 inhabitants, chiefly occupied in the smelting of copper and the export of metals—gold, silver, copper, cobalt, quicksilver, argentiferous lead, manganese, lead and iron being abundantly produced in the surrounding districts. Large quantities of skins and agricultural produce are also exported annually.

SERENA, the capital of the province, is 9 miles distant on the opposite side of the Bay. It is a fine and well-planned city of some 20,000 inhabitants, enjoying a very temperate and agreeable climate, and it lays claim to a certain amount of architectural grandeur, though the original city, founded in 1544, has been partly destroyed by fire and earthquakes on various occasions. It has still several buildings of note, a stately cathedral, several banks, and a fine central square and avenues; Serena is also one of the principal Bishop's Sees of Chile. Some two miles out of the town are the well-known copper mines of Brillador, together with the seigneurial estate of the proprietor.

A railway connects the town with Coquimbo, trains running each way three times daily. From Coquimbo there is an extension of the line to Olivo about 80 miles South, with a branch to the well-known copper mines of Panulcillo. The present terminus of the line is 12 miles from the capital town of Ovalle, whence a railway is under construction to the port of Tongoy, 27 miles South of Coquimbo. There is also a line running from Serena some 50 miles into the interior, up the Elqui valley.

Hotel accommodation both in Coquimbo and Serena is ample and rates are moderate.

The principal towns dependent on Coquimbo are:—

GUAYACAN, a small port about a mile distant from Coquimbo by land. The largest and best-found copper smelting establishment in Chile is situated here, and there are also extensive shops and brick factories. The output of bar copper is about 1,200 tons per month, in addition to considerable quantities of sulphate of copper.

TONGOY, a minor port 27 miles South, is also devoted to the copper industry, its smelting furnaces producing some 300 tons monthly.

OVALLE, chief town of the department of the same name, and situated in the valley of the Limari, is chiefly associated with the mining industry, though the vicinity is rich in agricultural products. Its population is about 16,000.

VICUÑA, chief town of the department of Elqui, has a population of 3,000; and is noted for its delightful climate, as well as for the wines, spirits, raisins and dried peaches produced in its vicinity.

ANDACOLLO, a village of some 400 inhabitants, distant about 30 miles, is remarkable for its rich deposits of gold and copper; as also for a very curious and time-honoured festival held there annually, in honour of the " Virgin of the Rosary," which brings together many thousands of persons from all parts of the Republic, as well as from the Argentine. The soil in this locality is said to be wonderfully rich in the precious metals, and promises lucrative results if systematically exploited—the washing process at present in use by the natives being of the most primitive description.

The interior valleys of the province of Coquimbo display a remarkable fertility and mineral wealth—from the coast to the Cordillera the country is traversed by rich veins of metals; cereals of all classes grow in abundance throughout the valleys, and the grape and other fruits are to be found in perfection. The communication with the interior is however bad, and the development which the province is capable of is much retarded in consequence. In most of the inland towns there is fair hotel accommodation.

Coquimbo possesses a telegraph cable station, and there is land wire communication with all the Chilian coast towns. Steamers southbound call every Monday and Friday; northbound, on Thursday and Sunday.

VALPARAISO is the chief port of Chile, and by far the most important maritime town on the coast. It has a population of about 100,000, a lively commerce, and an extensive though not always secure bay, which is visited by over a million tons of shipping annually. There is a fine esplanade running partly round the harbour for some 2½ miles, and a commodious iron pier provided with all modern appliances for working cargo.

The town is picturesquely situated at the foot of a range of steep hills, on a narrow stretch of land which from time to time has been reclaimed from the sea. In the business portion the streets are wide and regular, the houses and public edifices for the most part being well built and sightly. There are good services of tramways, telephones and electric light, several neatly arranged public gardens and squares, a stately opera house (the property of the town); some noble monuments, and various public buildings worthy of a visit.

The upper or suburban part of the town is built

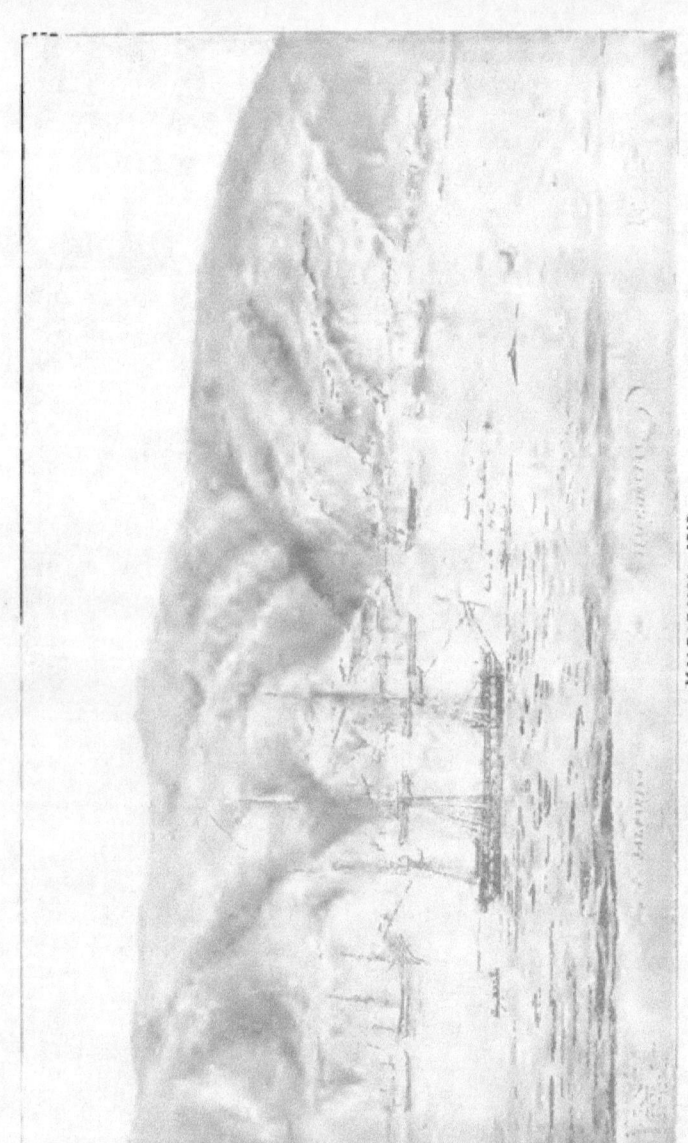

VALPARAISO, 1819.

on a succession of terraces, or ledges, leading up the face of the hills—and at some parts almost overhanging the lower town—as well as on the hill-top, and stretching away to the higher ranges in the background. These terraces are reached by a service of elevators, and by stairways and winding paths leading up the several ravines or chines in the hills. The climate of Valparaiso is healthy and bracing; particularly in the upper town, from which a commanding view is obtained. Hotel accommodation is ample and good, and at rates ranging from $3 currency per day.

Several notable peaks are visible from the bay, among which is Aconcagua, 22,420 feet.

SANTIAGO, the capital of the Republic, is pleasantly situated in the valley of the Mapocho, 115 miles by rail to the south-east of Valparaiso. Since the war with Peru, Santiago has considerably increased in importance as well as in beauty; and it now ranks as the finest city on the South Pacific Coast, comparing well with many European towns of greater pretensions. The population is about 200,000. The streets are wide, regular, and evenly arranged; the houses, laid out in square blocks, are well and solidly built, and of an architecture superior to that noticeable in other Coast towns. The public edifices are handsome and stately, the House of Representatives particularly being a very fine structure; whilst the San Carlos Gallery, President's Palace, Opera House, Alhambra, Cathedral, many of the churches, the Alameda, Cousiño Park, Municipal Gardens, and the many fine monuments of which the city boasts, may well be considered as of interest to the visitor. A fine view of Santiago and the surrounding country is to be obtained from the hill of Santa Lucia, which is situated almost in the centre of the city, and, being prettily laid out with winding pathways to the summit—where a restaurant and theatre are installed—is a popular pleasure resort. In the time of the conquest Santa Lucia was the Spanish stronghold, and the first settlers were held in siege there for over six months.

Santiago possesses a very complete system of tramways, electric light, telephones, and the most modern conveniences of civilisation. The hotel accommodation is all that could be desired, the principal establishments being—

Hotel Oddo   pension......... $4 to $5 per day.
    "   France ⎫
    "   Milan ⎬   " ......$3, $4 & $5   "
    "   Donay ⎭

Trains run between Valparaiso and Santiago twice a day each way; fare $6 currency, journey 5 hours.

The railways in this part of Chile are owned and worked by the State; considerable extensions are in project, though even now the system is the most complete on the coast. The trunk line, starting from Valparaiso, runs direct south from Santiago for some 400 miles, tapping the principal agricultural districts of this region—the inland towns of importance, as well as the principal coast ports, being in direct communication with the capital by means of branches connecting with the main line. It is the intention to continue this latter to Valdivia, an important agricultural centre, and the outlet for the extensive emigrant colonies of the province. A line is also in course of construction from Los Andes (90 miles east of Valparaiso) to Mendoza (Argentine Republic)—a direct transandine railroad from Valparaiso to Buenos Ayres. This line is, however, not likely to be completed for some years to come. At present the route is only practicable by mule tracks during the summer months, and even then is inclement and dangerous.

The principal places of interest in the vicinity of Valparaiso and Santiago are:

Vina Del Mar, a bathing station a few miles out of Valparaiso, much favoured by the people of the capital.

Limache, 28 miles from Valparaiso, on the line to Santiago; a prettily situated town and popular resort.

Quillota, the ancient capital of Chile, 40 miles inland of Valparaiso; population 5,000. The neighbourhood is famous for its fruits and vines.

San Felipe, about 90 miles from Valpariso, the capital of the department of Aconcagua; a neat and well-arranged town of 12,000 inhabitants. The surrounding country is rich in mineral and agricultural products.

Cauquenes Springs, a much frequented watering place 55 miles south of Santiago. The hydropathic establishment there is fairly-well installed, and the waters are held in high esteem.

Steamers leave Valparaiso for the north every Wednesday and Saturday; for the south once a week, and the P.S.N.C. Straits steamers sail fortnightly for the East Coast and Europe.

Constitucion is a thriving town about a mile up the river Maule. It is well built, and surrounded by a remarkably fertile country; but, owing to the difficulties in navigation of the river, its progress is greatly retarded: the present population is about 8,000. The principal exports are wine, wheat and other agricultural produce. There is a branch railway, 54 miles in extent, from Talca to Constitucion, on the main southern line from Santiago.

Talca, the chief town of the department, contains about 20,000 inhabitants, and carries on a considerable trade in agricultural products, wines, &c. There are some important flour mills in the town.

The Pacific Co. have a small steamer specially constructed for the traffic between Valparaiso and Constitucion, making trips at intervals of about five days.

TOMÉ, a small and prettily situated port on the bay of Concepcion, of some 4,000 inhabitants, is chiefly remarkable for the large quantities of excellent wine exported from the surrounding districts.

It has no railway communication, but is only a few miles distant from Constitucion.

The through mail, as well as the intermediate coast steamers, call at Tomé at frequent intervals.

TALCAHUANO is a rising port, situated in a fine and well sheltered bay, 240 miles south of Valparaiso. Population about 8000.

The Chilian Government is now building at Talcahuano extensive dry docks and breakwaters; and as it is intended to make a naval station there, it may be expected to become a place of considerable importance in course of time. At present it has a brisk commercial movement, is the principal port of shipment for the Southern wheat provinces, owns some large flour mills, and is in close proximity to the important town of Concepcion, to which it also serves as port. It is in direct railway communication with the capital and interior towns.

Concepcion, a few miles inland from Talcahuano, is the capital of Southern Chile. It is surrounded by some of the most fertile regions of the country, is a well arranged and pleasantly situated town of some 20,000 inhabitants, principally engaged in trade with the interior and the production of wines and preserved fruits. There are several large flour mills, and an important Government engineering establishment.

To the north of Concepcion, on the main line to Santiago, is the town of Chillan (16,000 inhabitants), which carries on a thriving trade in wine, cereals, and other agricultural produce.

At **Penco**, on the bay of Concepcion, and nine miles from the town, an important sugar refinery has been established. This small port is built on the site of the original city of Concepcion, destroyed in the great earthquake of 1835. There is a railway from Concepcion to Penco.

The P.S.N.C. Straits steamers call regularly at Talcahuano, both on the outward and homeward voyages. The through coast mail steamers, as well as those of the South Chilian coast line, also call regularly each way, and at frequent intervals. There is telegraphic communication with all the coast and inland towns.

CORONEL is essentially an industrial town, owing its present commercial status to the extensive coal deposits in the vicinity, the opening up of which, on a large scale, of late years has brought the place to a position of considerable importance among the Chilian coast towns. It is well situated in a deep and sheltered bay 40 miles south of Talcahuano, has ample mole accommodation, and, being the principal coaling station on the coast, is largely visited by shipping. The town itself is substantial in structure, and pleasing in appearance, having a population of 4000.

Up to within a recent date the principal coal workings have been along the sea shore, owing to the difficulty of transit from the interior; and some of these are still being exploited, producing coal of good quality, though having to be got from veins deep under the bay. The extended railway communication, however, now permits of the opening up, and profitable working, of vast tracts of almost virgin country, extremely rich both in coal and timber particularly the Colico district—and it is considered that a great future is in store for the Arauco coalfields and this region in general. The annual output of the various workings may be roughly put down as follows:

 The Arauco Company, 300,000 tons.
 The Lota Company, 200,000 tons.
 Messrs. Schwager and Company, 100,000 tons.
 Messrs. Rojas, 75,000 tons.

The Arauco Coal and Railway Company have a line from

Concepcion through Coronel, Lota, Colico, and all the principal coal districts, to Curanilahue, a distance of 62 miles. This line includes a remarkable bridge, 1,889 metres long, over the River Bio Bio, near Concepcion. There is also a narrow gauge line from Laraquete (a small coaling port four miles south of Lota) to the Carampangue mines.

Coronel possesses several engineering shops, and some large brick factories; the quality of the bricks and fire clay produced being much esteemed along the coast. Considerable quantities of copper are also exported yearly from the Lota Company's mines.

The port of **Lota**, five miles to the south of Coronel, is a small town of 5,000 inhabitants, chiefly engaged in the working and shipping of coal and copper. The gardens of Lota—a charmingly laid-out park, with mansion, the property of Mdme. Cousiño—are an interesting feature of the place.

The P.S.N.C. Straits steamers call regularly at Coronel both ways, as do also the through Panama-Valparaiso and the South Chilian Coast steamers; the two latter lines also touch at Lota regularly. There is telegraph communication from Coronel with all parts.

LEBÚ is a port of some consideration, 55 miles to the south of Coronel. It has risen in importance of late years, chiefly owing to the opening up of the extensive coal mines in the vicinity of the port, though the surrounding country is also rich in agricultural products. Large quantities of bark for tanning purposes are exported regularly.

The town of Lebú is in close proximity to the port, and at the mouth of the Lebú River. It has a population of 7,000, and is the capital of the province.

The steamers on the South Chilian coast line call at this port once a week each way.

VALDIVIA, on the river of the same name and four miles from its mouth, though but a small town of some 7,000 inhabitants, may be considered as a fairly important commercial centre, possessing several breweries and tanneries, the products of which are exported in considerable quantities. The province of Valdivia has been set apart for the German and Swiss emigrant colonies, and its population is said to be over 40,000. So far this region has not made the progress it is capable of, owing to the want of railway communication, which, however, it is intended to establish in the near future. There is fair hotel accommodation in Valdivia at from $2.50 to $3 per day.

Corral, the seaport of Valdivia, is situated at the mouth of the river. Traffic between Corral and Valdivia is carried on by a service of small river steamers.

The through steamers call at Corral four times a month each way, and the intermediate steamers once a week each way.

PORT MONTT, the principal port of the Chiloe Archipelago, is a neat and industrious town, with a population of some 3,000, enjoying a bracing and healthy climate. It is chiefly occupied in trade with the neighbouring islands and in the export of timber, the product of the dense virgin forests with which this part of the coast is covered. Fifteen miles from the port there is a German settlement, on the banks of Lake Llanquihue. There are many interesting places in the neighbourhood for excursionists, and horses and coaches are readily obtainable at moderate prices. There is also a steamboat running on the lake. Hotel accommodation is fair, and at customary rates.

Calbuco and Ancud, minor ports in the neighbourhood of Port Montt, also export large quantities of timber, and are called at regularly by the Valparaiso Coast steamer.

Port Montt is the southern terminus of the Pacific Co.'s Coast Line, and there are sailings from the port every week. There is also a service of small steamers running between the various islands and the port.

CHAPTER IX.

Approximate Values of the various South American Currencies.

The South American Republics having mainly a silver standard, it is impossible to give an actual sterling equivalent, owing to the fluctuations from time to time in the value of that metal, and also to the course of exchange. In Brazil especially the fluctuation is frequent and sometimes severe. The gold coinage, where it exists, is of course of full value.

For the information of travellers we append a list of the moneys in circulation and the present sterling values :—

Brazil. Gold : 20 milreis
10 ,,
5 ,,
2½ ,,
} 2s 3d per milreis.

Silver : 2000 reis
1000 ,,
500 ,,
200 ,,
100 ,,
50 ,,
} 9½d per milreis.

Paper of various denominations, 9½d per milreis.

Uruguay.—This is perhaps the only South

American country which maintains the silver coinage at face value, and the variation in exchange is very slight. The money consists of—

Silver : Peso.
50 centisimos
20 ,,
10 ,,
5 ,,
} 4s 2d per peso.

Paper of various denominations, 4s 2d per peso.

Argentina.—Gold 5 peso piece (Argentinos), £1.

Silver : Peso.
50 centavos
20 ,,
10 ,,
5 ,,
} 2s per peso.

Chile.—The Government of Chile have this year re-arranged their coinage with the view of establishing a fixed rate of exchange of 1s 6d per peso. The new gold coins are—

Condor, $20 = 30s.
Doblon, $10 = 15s.
Escudo, $5 = 7s 6d.

Silver : Peso.
50 centavos
20 ,,
10 ,,
5 ,,
} 1s 6d per peso.

It was anticipated that the paper money would maintain a fixed rate of 18d per peso, but the present value is slightly under par. The gold ounce is still in circulation to a small extent—value 16 pesos.

Bolivia.—Gold : Ounce — 16 pesos, £3 3s 0d.
4 pesos, 15s 9d.

Silver : Peso.
50 centavos } 2s per peso.
20   „

Peru.—Gold : 20 soles
10   „ } 3s 10d per sol.
5   „

Silver : Sol.
50 centavos
20   „   } 2s per sol.
10   „
5   „

Ecuador.—Silver :

Sucre
20 centavos } 2s per sucr.

Colombia.—Gold : 10 pesos, 3s 8d per peso.

Silver : Peso
50 centavos } 2s per peso.

Money of all descriptions is received on board the Pacific Co.'s steamers in payment of fares, wine accounts &c., at values which may be ascertained from the pursers.

PACIFIC LINE.

TO BRAZIL, RIVER PLATE AND ALL PORTS ON THE WEST COAST OF SOUTH AMERICA.

The Pacific Steam Navigation Co.'s Steamers

Are appointed to sail from **LIVERPOOL** with Her Majesty's Mails

Every Alternate Thursday

FOR

RIO DE JANEIRO, MONTE VIDEO (FOR BUENOS AYRES), PUNTA ARENAS (STRAITS OF MAGELLAN),

AND THE

WEST COAST OF SOUTH AMERICA,

CALLING TO LAND AND EMBARK PASSENGERS AT

LA PALLICE (LA ROCHELLE), CORUNNA, VIGO, LEIXOES (OPORTO), and LISBON.

EVERY ALTERNATE STEAMER TOUCHING AT

PERNAMBUCO AND BAHIA.

Also Monthly Line of fast Cargo Steamers to East and West Coasts.

THROUGH BOOKINGS TO AND FROM THE PACIFIC,

Via New York, San Francisco, Colon and Panama,

In conjunction with the undermentioned Lines, according to route —

WHITE STAR LINE.	**WEST INDIA & PACIFIC S.S. CO.**
PACIFIC MAIL LINE.	**HARRISON LINE.**
PANAMA STEAM-SHIP CO.	**CIE GLE TRANSATLANTIQUE.**
ROYAL MAIL S.S. CO.	**CIA. TRASATLANTICA de BARCELONA**
LA VELOCE NAVIGAZIONE ITALIANA	**PRINCE LINE**
HAMBURG-AMERICAN STEAM PACKET CO.	

Reduced Fares and Special Terms for Return Tickets and for Families.

PACIFIC LINE.

TOURS IN THE PYRENEES

AND

South of France.

A Set of Eighteen different Tours have been arranged by The Pacific Steam Navigation Co., ranging in price from

£6 6s 0d to £13 9s 0d.

The Fares include Maintenance and free table Wine (Claret) on board Steamer. The Tickets for the complete Tour, i.e., using the Company's Steamers out and home, are available for two months.

Further Particulars may be had on application to any of the Company's Agents, or to the

HEAD OFFICE,

31 JAMES STREET,

LIVERPOOL

ORIENT LINE.

FORTNIGHTLY MAIL SERVICE
BETWEEN
ENGLAND & AUSTRALIA.

	Tons Reg.	H.P.		Tons Reg.	H.P.
AUSTRAL	5,524	7,000	ORIZABA	6,077	7,000
CUZCO	3,898	4,000	ORMUZ	6,031	8,500
LUSITANIA	3,877	4,000	OROTAVA	5,552	7,000
OPHIR	6,910	10,000	OROYA	6,057	7,000
ORIENT	5,365	6,000	ORUBA	5,552	7,000

Calling to land and embark passengers at **Gibraltar, Naples, Port Said, Ismailia, Suez, Colombo, Albany, Adelaide, Melbourne,** and **Sydney.**

Through Tickets to all other Ports in **Australia, Tasmania,** and **New Zealand.**

High-class cuisine, electric lighting, hot and cold baths, good ventilation, and every comfort.

FARES TO AUSTRALIA FROM £15 15 - TO £70.
Cheap Return Tickets, and for Tours Round the World.

Managers { F. GREEN & CO. / ANDERSON, ANDERSON & CO. } Fenchurch Avenue, London, E.C.

For Passage apply in LONDON to the latter firm at
5 FENCHURCH AVENUE, E.C.

Or to the WEST END Branch Office,
16 COCKSPUR STREET, S.W.

In LIVERPOOL to
THE PACIFIC STEAM NAVIGATION CO., 31 JAMES STREET.

WHITE STAR LINE
ROYAL MAIL STEAMERS,
LIVERPOOL TO NEW YORK,
Every WEDNESDAY,
Calling at QUEENSTOWN for Mails and Passengers.

The Magnificent Twin Screw Steamers **Majestic** and **Teutonic**, each 10,000 Tons, sail regularly in the itinerary of the Line.

SALOON FARES.
"MAJESTIC" AND "TEUTONIC."

Winter Season ......(From 1st November)...£12, £15, £18, £20 & £25 per berth
Summer   „   ....(From 15th July)......£18, £20, £25, £30 & £35   „
Deck Rooms from £50 and upwards for Winter Season, and from £80 and upwards for Summer Season, according to schedule.

"BRITANNIC," "GERMANIC" AND "ADRIATIC."

Winter Season ....(From 1st November)............£10 10/-, £12, £15 & £20.
Summer   „   ....(From 15th July) ....£12, £15, £20 & £25,
according to position of berth and number in State Room, all having equal privileges in the Saloon.

Children under Twelve years, Half-Fare. Infants under Two years, Free.

RETURN RATES.—Ten per cent off combined Outward and Homeward Fares, according to Season, except at the £12 rate by *Majestic* and *Teutonic*, and at £10 10/- by other Steamers.

SECOND CABIN, £8 to £10. RETURN, £15 to £18, according to Steamer and Season.

☞ Steerage Passage (including Outfit) to New York, Boston, or Philadelphia at low rates.

THROUGH BOOKINGS
Between SOUTH AMERICAN PORTS and NEW YORK, via LIVERPOOL, By Pacific Steam Navigation Co.'s and White Star Line Steamers, at Reduced rates.

APPLY TO
JAMES SCOTT & CO., Queenstown; H. GENESTAL & DELZONS, 1 Ru Scribe, Paris; H. MAITLAND KERSEY, 29 Broadway, New York, or to ISMAY, IMRIE & CO., 34 Leadenhall Street, London, and 10 Water Street, Liverpool.

THE GRAND CENTRAL.

TRUNK LINE of the ARGENTINE REPUBLIC conn[ecting] with the ANDINE, G.W. ARG., and other Railways to [the] WEST COAST, and the principal routes to TUCUMAN, SAL[TA,] JUJUY, and on the North generally.

Travellers by this Line pass through the richest Gra[zing] and Grain Fields of the Country, and can travel direct [to] the most picturesque sections and popular health resort[s,] COSQUIN, CRUZ DEL EJE, ALTA GRACIA, ROSARIO DE [LA] FRONTERA, &c.

The Line is fully equipped with all the necessary [and] latest improvements for the comfort, convenience and saf[ety] of Travellers, luxurious Sleeping and Dining Coaches, [and] Smoking Cars, being a prominent feature of the service.

Special Booking arrangements have been made with [the] principal Steam-ship Companies, whereby Tourists may obt[ain] all needed information and attention previous to landing [at] Buenos Aires or Rosario.

Particular information as to Tickets, Routes, Point[s of] Interest, &c., may be obtained at the District Office, 460 C[alle] Piedad, Buenos Aires, or at the Office of the Traffic Super[in]tendent in Rosario.

London Offices, 85 Palmerston Buildings, Bishopsgate Str[eet.]

THE Buenos Aires & Rosario Railway.

THE BUENOS AIRES & ROSARIO RAILWAY is the principal line in the Argentine Republic running Northward from Buenos Aires to the important provinces of **SANTA FÉ, CORDOBA, SANTIAGO DEL ESTERO** and **TUCUMAN**, and connecting those districts and the Cities of **SALTA** and **JUJUY** (on the Central Northern Line) with the Federal Capital.

The Railway, after traversing the maize-growing region of Buenos Aires province, arrives at Rosario, the second largest centre of commerce in the country, where it has goods depôts, warehouses, elevators and shoots, sidings, &c., on an elaborate scale, for the purpose of dealing with the enormous traffic which it conveys to that important port on the River Paraná.

The wheat-producing area of the province of Santa Fé is also served by this Line, as are the sugar plantations and the forests of Tucuman and Santiago, the annual yield of which is rapidly increasing.

The comforts of passengers by this Railway have been studied to such an extent that, with its excellent train service, its luxurious dining and smoking saloons, and commodious sleeping cars, as well as its ordinary coaching stock, all of which have been arranged and fitted in the most modern and artistic style, it has attained the celebrity of being the best ordered Line in the country.

THOMAS COOK & SON,

Originators of the European Tourist and Excursion System.

ESTABLISHED 1841.

COOK'S INTERNATIONAL TRAVELLING TICKETS are available for one or more passengers to travel by any trains any day, and do not compel the holders to travel in parties.

AMERICAN TOURS.—Messrs. Thomas Cook and Son issue Tickets to all parts of America and Canada.

AUSTRALIA AND NEW ZEALAND.—Under special arrangements with the Australasian Railway Administrations, Thomas Cook and Son issue Tickets to and through all parts of these countries.

EGYPT AND THE HOLY LAND.—Cook's Eastern Tours are the result of many years' study and practical investigation, and are the most popular of all arrangements for visiting Bible Lands.

HOLLAND, BELGIUM, THE RHINE, GERMANY, AUSTRIA, &c.—Thomas Cook and Son issue their own Tickets for Single or Return Journeys, or Circular Tours, including all places of interest.

INDIA, CHINA, &c.—Tickets issued to any point, and through special contracts with the Indian Government, Tourist Tickets can be had for all parts of India.

ITALY.—Single Journey and Circular Tickets to and through all parts of Italy.

NILE, THE STEAM NAVIGATION OF THE.—Thomas Cook and Son (Egypt), Ltd., are the sole owners of the New Tourist Steamers on the Nile, and Tickets can be had and berths secured at any of their Offices.

PARIS.—Cook's Single and Return Tickets by the Mail Route, *vid* Dover and Calais. Hotel accommodation at cheapest rates. Through Interpreters and Carriage Drives in Paris.

SWITZERLAND.—Cook's Swiss Tickets embrace every Railway, Steamer and Diligence Route in the country, and are issued at greatly reduced fares.

HOTEL COUPONS.—The system of Hotel Coupons introduced by Thomas Cook and Son reduces the troubles of Continental travel to a minimum. The coupons are issued at a uniform rate, and are accepted at first class hotels in all parts of the World.

PERSONALLY CONDUCTED TOURS under efficient management leave London at frequent intervals. For full particulars apply at any of the Tourist Offices.

BANKING AND EXCHANGE.—Foreign Money of all denominations bought and sold. Bank Drafts. Circular notes issued and Cable Transfers made, &c.

OCEAN PASSAGE TICKETS TO ALL PARTS OF THE GLOBE, by all Lines of Steamers, at lowest rates.

THOMAS COOK & SON,
Chief Office: Ludgate Circus, LONDON.

MIDLAND GRAND HOTEL,
LONDON, N.W.

The **Midland Grand** is the finest and largest Hotel in London. It is within shilling Cab Fare of nearly all Theatres and Business and West End centres; close to King's Cross Metropolitan Station. Buses to all parts every minute.

The **Midland Grand** has a large free area all round it, and being well ventilated and properly warmed in winter it is a desirable residence for Ladies and Families coming to town for either a long or short visit.

LADIES' & FAMILY COFFEE ROOM on First Floor *en suit*, with Music, Drawing, Writing and Reading Rooms.

PASSENGER ELEVATORS.

ELECTRIC LIGHT EVERYWHERE.

REFINEMENT AND COMFORT.

BEDROOMS.—For one person from 4/-; for two persons from 5/6. (No charge for Attendance and Electric Light.)

BREAKFAST.—Table d'Hôte, consisting of Tea, Coffee, or Chocolate, Porridge and Cream, several kinds of Fish and Meat, Cold Viands, &c., served from 8 to 10-30 a.m. 3 0

LUNCHEON.— Table d'Hôte Express Luncheon, 1 to 2-30 p.m. 3 0

DINNER. Table d'Hôte (high-class French Cuisine), 6-30 to 8 p.m. 5 0

Home Dinner (Five Courses), at 6 p.m., Sundays 5-30 p.m. 3 6

THE NEW VENETIAN ROOMS are now available for Wedding Breakfasts, At Homes, Receptions, and other public and private functions.

Hotels under same Management:—

MIDLAND, BRADFORD.
(A model Hotel.)
Electric Light everywhere, Passengers Lift, Restaurant, Café.

MIDLAND, DERBY.
For Peak of Derbyshire, Haddon Hall, Chatsworth, &c.

QUEEN'S, LEEDS.
Adjoins the Midland, North-Eastern, and London and North-Western Stations, in the centre of the town.

MIDLAND, MORECAMBE.
Convenient for English Lakes.

Tariffs on Application. Telegraphic Address to each Hotel: "Midotel."

WILLIAM TOWLE, Manager.

For **ADELPHI HOTEL, LIVERPOOL** (under same Management) see opposite page.

ADELPHI HOTEL, LIVERPOOL

(The Hotel de Luxe of the North).

The ADELPHI HOTEL is close to the Central (Midland) Station, and within 15 minutes' walk of the Docks: has undergone an entire reconstruction of internal arrangements, and is now one of the most completely-arranged Hotels in the world.

The accommodation includes—

Telephones.—Telephone in every Apartment, enabling Visitors to send orders to the respective Departments of the Hotel, or to communicate direct with their friends in other parts of the house.

Electric Light.—Electric Light everywhere.

Elevators.—Rapid Passenger Lift to each floor.

Library.—There is a Library for the use of Visitors, without charge.

Louis XV. Restaurant.—Visitors will find the Louis XV. Restaurant arranged for the à la Carte service of highest-class French Cuisine.

Steam Laundry and Hair-Dressing Saloons. There is a Steam Laundry in the Hotel, and also Ladies' and Gentlemen's Hair-Dressing Saloons.

Bedroom. For one person from 4/-; for two persons from 5/6. No charge for Attendance and Electric Light.

Breakfast.—Table d'Hôte, consisting of Tea, Coffee, or Chocolate, Porridge and Cream, several kinds of Fish and Meat, Cold Viands, &c., served from 8 to 10-30 a.m., 3/-.

Luncheon.—Home Luncheon served from 12 to 3 p.m., 3/-.

Dinner.—Table d'Hôte (high-class French Cuisine) served from 6 to 8 p.m., 5/-. Dinners à la Carte or at fixed prices, from 3/-.

The ADELPHI, with its comfort and homeliness and repose to be found there, is a suitable resting place for Transatlantic Travellers on either the homeward or outward journey.

TARIFFS ON APPLICATION.   Telegraphic Address: "MIDOTEL."

WILLIAM TOWLE, Manager.

Chief Office: Midland Grand Hotel, London, N.W.

For other MIDLAND RAILWAY HOTELS, see opposite page.

HOTEL ORIENTAL

This splendid and commodious Hotel, situated in the Calle Solis, is considered by many English and American travellers to be the finest Hotel in South America.

The cuisine is excellent, the general arrangements of the Hotel and the apartments are of a first-class order, whilst the charges are moderate.

Private Sitting Rooms, if desired, can be obtained for a small extra charge.

The Hotel is elegantly furnished, and is replete with every modern comfort and convenience.

HOTEL ORIENTAL
MONTE VIDEO.

HOTEL SUL-AMERICANO,

PRAÇA CASTRO ALVES,

Telegraph Address: "AMERICANO."
Telephone No. 342.

BAHIA, BRAZIL.

This first-class Hotel occupies the finest and most central position in Bahia. It is within five minutes walk of the Theatre. Cars for all parts of the City pass in close proximity. It contains a spacious Drawing Room, Reading Room, Coffee Room and Billiard Room, and is well adapted for Banquets, &c., &c.

The Hotel, which was opened in January, 1895, has been built in accordance with the necessities of the climate of the country, the rooms being large and well ventilated.

Bath Rooms, &c. (hot and cold) on every Floor.

PRICES.—8$000 and 10$000 per day.
        Breakfast 3$000 and Dinner 3$500.
        Special arrangements can be made for families.

Estabeleciment de primeira classe em toda America do Sul inaugurado em Janeiro 1895.

Com edificio construido de accordo com o clima do paiz, collocado no centro da cidade e linha de viação com toda o conforto para viajantes e familias, tendo boas habitações e as melhores condicções hygienicas.

Salões para recepção dos hospedes para banquetes, bilhares e maissallas destinadas a refeições.

Serviço completo de lavanderia, quartos bem mobilados, barbeiros, e cosinha franceza.

PREÇOS—Pensão diaria 8$000 & 10$000.
        Almoço extra 3$000. Jantar extra 3$500.
        Para as familias grandes, e creanças ha abatimento nos preços.

Proprietors: ALVES & IRMAO. Manager: ARLINDO ALVES.

Grande Hotel Metropole

Rua das Larangeiras N. 181
TELEPHONE 5026.

Healthiest Suburb of the city.	Bairro saluberrimo.
The most comfortable for families and travellers.	O mais confortavel para familias e viajantes.
Tram cars at any time.	Bonds a toda hora.
Excellent Restaurant.	Restaurante excellente.
Wines and liqueurs of every description.	Vinhos e licores de todas os qualidades.
Shower and warm baths.	Banhos frios e quentes.

RIO DE JANEIRO.

THE "BRITISH" P.P. PAPER CO.
LONDON, ENGLAND.

THE LARGEST MANUFACTURERS OF TOILET ROLLS IN THE WORLD.

Illustrated List on application.

BANK OF LIVERPOOL LIMITED.

ESTABLISHED 1831.

Subscribed Capital, £8,000,000; of which Reserved, £4,800,000; Callable, £2,200,000; Paid Up, £1,000,000; Reserved Surplus Fund, £561,811 3/1.

BOARD OF DIRECTORS

FOR THE YEAR 1895-96.

THOS. BROCKLEBANK, Esq., J.P., CHAIRMAN.
ROBERT D. HOLT, Esq., J.P., DEPUTY CHAIRMAN.

W. D. CREWDSON, Esq., J.P.	ALFRED T. PARKER, Esq.
ARTHUR EARLE, Esq., J.P.	HUGH L. SMYTH, Esq., J.P.
E. H. HARRISON, Esq., J.P.	W. H. TATE, Esq., J.P.
CHARLES LANGTON, Esq., J.P.	JACOB WAKEFIELD, Esq., J.P.

JAMES M. WOOD, Esq.

HEAD OFFICE: 7 WATER STREET, LIVERPOOL.

J. HOPE SIMPSON	*General Manager.*
GEO. T. ADDIS	*Sub-Manager.*
FRANCIS W. CREWDSON	*District General Manager, Kendal.*
EDWARD W. WAKEFIELD	*Assistant District Manager, Kendal.*

32 BRANCHES AND 15 SUB-BRANCHES.

London Agents:

MESSRS. GLYN, MILLS, CURRIE & CO.	MESSRS. ROBARTS, LUBBOCK & CO.
MESSRS. BARCLAY, BEVAN & CO.	WILLIAMS, DEACON & MANCHESTER AND SALFORD BANK LTD.

Current and Deposit Accounts opened for Customers residing at home or abroad. Interest allowed on sums remaining for one month, at the rates for the time being of the leading London Joint Stock Banks.

The Bank acts as Agents for Home and Foreign Banks, and, through its Foreign connections, offers facilities for the transfer of money by cable.

Customers going abroad can have dividends received to their credit, and payments attended to during their absence; and documents of value may be left with the Bank for safe custody, at the Customer's risk.

The Bank has Agents and Correspondents in all the principal towns of Great Britain and Ireland, and on the Continent of Europe.

A few of its principal Correspondents in other countries are subjoined, for convenience of reference.

CANADA	Bank of Montreal. Bank of B. N. America.
UNITED STATES OF N. AMERICA	Bank of Montreal. Brown Brothers & Co. and various Banks throughout the states.
AUSTRALIA AND NEW ZEALAND	Bank of Australasia. Union Bank of Australia Limited. Bank of New Zealand.
SOUTH AFRICA	Standard Bank of South Africa Limited.
INDIA, CHINA AND THE EAST	Chartered Bank of India, Australia and China.
SOUTH AMERICA	London Bank of Mexico and S. America Limited. London and River Plate Bank Limited. Bank of Tarapacá and London Limited.
WEST INDIES	Colonial Bank.

LONDON AND BRAZILIAN BANK, LIMITED.

CAPITAL, £1,500,000, in 75,000 SHARES of £20 each.

Paid-up Capital, 75,000 Shares at £10 = £750,000.

Reserve Fund, £600,000.

HEAD OFFICE—8 TOKENHOUSE YARD, LONDON, E.C.

DIRECTORS.

HON. PASCOE CHARLES GLYN, Chairman.

CHARLES EDWARD JOHNSTON, Esq., Deputy-Chairman.

JOHN BEATON, Esq., Managing Director.
EDWARD LONSDALE BECKWITH, Esq.
CHARLES SEYMOUR GRENFELL, Esq.
WILLIAM DOURO HOARE, Esq.
WILLIAM WILTON PHIPPS, Esq.
CHARLES DAY ROSE, Esq.

EDMUND D. SCHLUTER, Esq.
JOHN GORDON, Esq., Manager.

BANKERS.

London—BANK OF ENGLAND.
Messrs. GLYN, MILLS, CURRIE & CO.

Paris—Messrs. MALLET FRÈRES & CO.

Hamburg—Messrs. SCHRÖDER & CO.
Messrs. JOH. BERENBERG, GOSSLER & CO.

BRANCHES: BRAZIL—Rio de Janeiro, Pernambuco, Bahia, Rio Grande do Sul, Pará, Santos, San Paulo, Pelotas, Porto Alegre. RIVER PLATE—Monte Video, Buenos Ayres. NEW YORK (Agency). PORTUGAL—Lisbon, Oporto.

CORRESPONDENTS: BRAZIL—Bage, Campinas, Campos, Ceará, Maceió, Manaós, Maranham, Natal, Parahyba, Santa Catharina. PORTUGAL—Amarante, Braga, Coimbra, Faro, Figueira, Guimarães, Lagos, Portimão, Setubal, Silves, Sines, Tavira, Vianna, Villa Real. RIVER PLATE—Paysandu, Rosario, San Nicolas.

THE LONDON & RIVER PLATE BANK,
LIMITED.

ESTABLISHED 1862.

Subscribed Capital............£1,500,000.

Paid up Capital, £900,000.   Reserve Fund, £900,000

Branches in—

PARIS, BUENOS AYRES, MONTE VIDEO, ROSARIO, RIO DE JANEIRO, PERNAMBUCO & PARÁ.

AGENCIES IN PAYSANDU & NEW YORK.

Letters of Credit, Drafts, and Cable Transfers issued. Bills negotiated, advanced upon or sent for collection.

7 Princes Street, E.C.   January, 1895.

LIMITED,

SHIPBUILDERS AND ENGINEERS,

BELFAST, IRELAND.

ON THE BRITISH ADMIRALTY LIST FOR MACHINERY AND WAR-SHIPS OF THE LARGEST CLASS. BUILDERS OF THE ENTIRE WHITE STAR FLEET; ALSO OF ALL ADDITIONS TO THE FLEET OF THE PACIFIC STEAM NAVIGATION COMPANY DURING THE PAST FOUR YEARS.

Winners of Gold and other Prize Medals. Eleven in Number.

BRINTONS, LIMITED,
KIDDERMINSTER.
MANUFACTURERS OF
BRUSSELS, WILTON, PATENT TUFTED AXMINSTER, CAIRO SQUARES AND OTHER

CARPETS & RUGS.

WOOL COMBERS AND WORSTED SPINNERS.

Works and Registered Office - KIDDERMINSTER

WAREHOUSES
London 61 Holborn Viaduct, E.C.
Leicester Atlas Chambers, Berridge Street.
Paris 18 rue des Petites-Ecuries.
Berlin 33a Franzosischestrasse I Etage W 56.
Canada 162 St. James Street, Montreal.
British Columbia Turner Block, Cordova Street, Vancouver.
South Africa 31 Castle Street, Cape Town.
Australia Mr. A. A. Boyd, Melbourne.

R. R. MINTON & CO.
CHEAPSIDE PAINT WORKS,
LIVERPOOL.

MANUFACTURERS OF

PAINTS, COLORS & VARNISHES
FOR ALL CLIMATES,
OIL BOILERS AND REFINERS,

CONTRACTORS TO ADMIRALTY,
INDIA OFFICE and
CROWN AGENTS TO COLONIES.

Branches : MANCHESTER, LEEDS and CARDIFF.

USED ON RECORD TRIPS.

CRANE'S OILS

FOR

ENGINES AND CYLINDERS.

"Absolutely the BEST."

TRADE MARKS.

Over Forty Years' Reputation.

Used by
The Pacific Steam Navigation Co., The Orient Line,
— The Union Line, —
The Castle Line, The Compagnie General Trasatlantique
The Hamburg and American Steam Shipping Co.,
and The Principal Steamship Companies in the World.

Direct from the Sole Manufacturers—

P. MOIR CRANE & CO.
Bank Street, MANCHESTER.

Stocks kept for Prompt Delivery at

LIVERPOOL	... ...	21 Water Street.
LONDON...	...	29 Fenchurch Street, E.C.
CARDIFF...		...5 Mount Stuart Square.
GLASGOW	...	... 17 Oswald Street.

CLARKE, CHAPMAN & CO. LTD.

ENGINEERS,

GATESHEAD-ON-TYNE.

MAKERS OF

ALL CLASSES OF SHIPS' DECK MACHINERY.

ELECTRIC INSTALLATIONS

BOTH FOR

LAND AND SHIP LIGHTING.

Electric Transmission of Power,

MOTORS FOR VARIOUS PURPOSES.

OIL ENGINES,

Silent, Simple, Economical, Durable, specially adapted for Electric Installations and Agricultural Work.

STEAM PUMPING MACHINERY.

Telegraphic Address "CYCLOPS, GATESHEAD."

TO MERCHANTS AND SHIPPERS ONLY.

JACKSON, McCONNAN & TEMPLE,

LIVERPOOL, ENGLAND,

Manufacturers of Hemp Cordage of all descriptions and sizes, And Spinners of Binder Twines.

Best White Manila Rope.
Best White Sisal Rope.
New Zealand Hemp Rope.
Coir or Cocoa Rope, made from selected Yarns.
Cotton Rope for Machine Driving, &c.
White Russian Hemp Rope.
Tarred Russian Hemp Cordage.
Tarred Russian Hemp Boltrope, Marline, Spunyarn, Houseline and Amberline.
Flax and Hemp Spunyarn for Engineers' use.
Manila Binder Twine.
Sisal Binder Twine.
Manila and Sisal Cords for Hay Banding, &c.

ALSO,

All descriptions of Log and Deep Sea Lines, and Signal Halyards, plaited and plain.
Machine and Hand-picked Oakum.

All of the best quality and manufacture.

WORKS: EDGE LANE, near LIVERPOOL.

ROSS'S ROYAL
"BELFAST"
AERATED TABLE WATERS

As Supplied for many years to

Pacific Steam Navigation Co.; West India Royal Mail; Shaw, Saville and Albion; Cunard; White Star; International and many other first-class Steam Packet Companies.

"SAFEST DRINKS IN ANY CLIMATE.

Prepared in apparatus of Earthenware, Slate, Glass and Silver, thus preventing metallic impregnation. Water is obtained on the premises from a beautiful Spring 226 feet deep.

(Prepared and Packed to suit all Climates.)

Are recognised STANDARDS of EXCELLENCE wherever IMPORTED AERATED WATERS are known or used.

Enquire specially for our world-renowned **GINGER ALE** at all first-class Wine Merchants, Chemists, Grocers, Hotels, and Restaurants; also on board Passenger Steamers to all parts of the World.

LATEST HONOURS.

THESE DRINKS OBTAINED THE HIGHEST AWARDS AT THE
CHICAGO EXPOSITION, 1893.

They are recommended by the Faculty, the Medical Journals and the most eminent Analytical Chemists of the day.

W. A. ROSS & SONS, LIMITED,
AERATED WATER MANUFACTURERS,
BELFAST.

"Johannis"
The King of Natural Table Waters.

Supplied under Royal Warrant to Her Majesty the Queen.

A pure Water sparkling with its own Natural Gas.

JOHANNIS prevents Gout, Rheumatism, Sea Sickness and Indigestion.

JOHANNIS blends equally well with Wines, Spirits or Milk.

JOHANNIS makes a grand Lemon Squash.

All residents in hot climates should make JOHANNIS their standard drink, as a safeguard against Typhoid Fever and the many Stomach Complaints brought about by impure water.

In Tropical Countries were JOHANNIS has already found its way, repeat orders have invariably followed.

Carried by all the principal Steam-ship Companies.

Springs–Zollhaus, Germany.

PROPRIETORS:
JOHANNIS, Limited, 25 Regent Street, London, S.W.

Liverpool Office & Stores, 46 Hanover Street.

Telegrams: "Waste, Stockport." Established 1828.

R. H. HAMPSON,

EGERTON MILLS,

STOCKPORT,

Near MANCHESTER, ENGLAND.

Manufacturer of ENGINE WASTE, SPONGE CLOTHS, WICKINGS, and HORTICULTURAL SHADINGS; Also COTTON and COTTON WASTE MERCHANT, HOME, COLONIAL, and FOREIGN GOVERNMENT and RAILWAY STORES CONTRACTOR.

Under Contract with The Pacific Steam Navigation Co. for Engine Waste, &c., and other Steamship Companies; also with the Railway Companies in Great Britain and Ireland.

MACKENZIE & MACKENZIE,
EDINBURGH.

BISCUIT MANUFACTURERS
TO
Her Majesty and Royal Family.

MAKERS OF THE CELEBRATED
Albert, Wheaten,
Cream Crackers,
Extra Toast,
AND
Rich Mixed Biscuits,
ALSO
SCOTCH SHORTBREAD,
OATCAKES, Etc., Etc.

STAMINA MALT AND GOLF BISCUITS.

Latest specialties, with delicious flavour and strengthening and sustaining properties.

TELEGRAMS:
"SODIUM."

TELEPHONE
No. 700.

J. H. & S. JOHNSON,
6, 8 & 10 WHITECHAPEL,
2 and 3 LEIGH STREET,
LIVERPOOL.

Wholesale Druggists, Oil Merchants,
DRYSALTERS,
AND
PAINT MANUFACTURERS.

FINE FRENCH COLZA OIL.
CRYSTAL OIL,

For burning in Paraffin Lamps. Will give a brilliant flame, free from unpleasant smell, and is quite safe with ordinary care.

MARINE ENGINE OILS.
MACHINERY OILS
Of Every Description.

DISINFECTANTS.
CARBOLIC ACID, CHLORIDE OF LIME, CONDY'S FLUID,
CARBOLIC POWDER, AND PERMANGANATE OF POTASH.

Chemical and Scientific Apparatus. Analytical Balances.

Importers of German Glass and Berlin Porcelain Ware,
And Graduated Glasses.

ESTIMATES given for Fitting up Laboratories to any required extent.

CORROSIVE ACID PACKED FOR EXPORT.

PHOTOGRAPHIC CHEMICALS & APPARATUS,
For Home use and for Exportation.

MEDICINE CHESTS FITTED COMPLETE FOR ALL CLIMATES.

Established 1843.

PORT GLASGOW & NEWARK
SAILCLOTH CO.

CONTRACTORS TO THE ADMIRALTY.

Manufacturers of

FLAX & COTTON

SAILCLOTH

VARIOUS QUALITIES.

WATERPROOF CANVAS,

TARPAULINGS,

FILTER CLOTHS AND SHEATH CLOTHS.

MACHINE SAIL TWINES,

SEAMING AND ROPING TWINES, &c.

WORKS: **PORT GLASGOW, SCOTLAND.**

Telegrams:—"NEWARK, PORT GLASGOW."

QUIGGIN'S PATENTED SPECIALITIES.

Cablegrams per Scott's Code—
"ELIMINATOR, LIVERPOOL."

EVAPORATORS
FOR
PRODUCING PURE WATER,

External Heater,
CAST IRON TYPE.

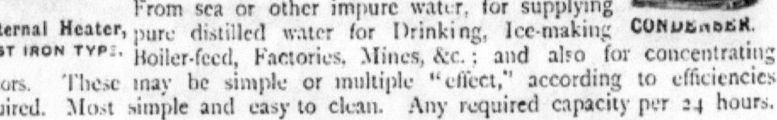

CONDENSER.

From sea or other impure water, for supplying pure distilled water for Drinking, Ice-making, Boiler-feed, Factories, Mines, &c.; and also for concentrating liquors. These may be simple or multiple "effect," according to efficiencies required. Most simple and easy to clean. Any required capacity per 24 hours.

FRESH WATER CONDENSERS

of any size to produce cold filtered water from steam. Simple and sure.

FEED-WATER HEATERS

of External or Internal types, made in cast iron or wrought steel, for any pressure or power. Worked either with live or exhaust steam.

FEED-WATER FILTERS

of most improved and latest design. Easily cleaned and most effective.

☞ These Specialities have been supplied to all the leading Steam-Ship Companies, including the Pacific Co., Cunard Co., White Star Co., American Line,

Lamport & Holt.
R. Singlehurst & Co.
Harland & Wolff.
Dennys.
Thomsons, Clydebank.
Fairfield Co.
Laird Bros., &c. &c.
ALSO THE
English Navy.
Argentine   ,,
Italian   ,,
Indian Marine, &c. &c.

For Prices, &c., apply to

The Liverpool Engineering and Condenser Company, Ltd.
SOLE MAKERS,
BRASENOSE ROAD,
LIVERPOOL, ENGLAND.

EVAPORATOR
TYPE B.—*Showing Coils removed.*

EVAPORATOR
Fitted also to work as When Exhaust Condenser.—TYPE A.

JOHN A. BREMNER & CO.

Albert Street, Manchester, and 79 Mark Lane, London

MANUFACTURERS OF

OILS LUBRICATING OILS

FOR

MARINE AND STATIONARY ENGINES

AND

ALL CLASSES OF MACHINERY.

SPECIAL CYLINDER & VALVE OIL

CARDIFF,   LIVERPOOL,
BUTE DOCKS.   OLD CHURCH YARD

GLASGOW,   NEWCASTLE-ON-TYNE
YORK STREET.   41 SANDHILL.

The above are largely in use by leading consumers, including—

THE PACIFIC STEAM NAVIGATION CO.
THE CUNARD CO. LTD.
Messrs. PLATT BROS. & CO. LTD., OLDHAM,
Messrs. HOWARD & BULLOUGH, LTD., ACCRINGTON
And many other well-known firms.

CYLINDER OILS as supplied to the English Admiralty

WEIRS'
BOILER-FEEDING SPECIALTIES.

Marine Feed-Water Heaters,
With Central Gear for Feed Pumps.

Surface Feed-Water Heaters.
Largest and Most Efficient Surface in Minimum Space.

Direct-Acting Feed Pumps.
Latest and Most Approved Design.

EVAPORATORS.
Capacity from 2 to 50 Tons per day.
Simplest, Most Efficient and Best in the Market.

Combination Feed & Blow-off Cock.
Saves Joints and Connections.

Hydrokineters, for Boiler Circulation.

Adopted by the leading Steamship Companies, and by the British, Austro-Hungarian, Chilian, Chinese, Dutch, French, Italian, Japanese, Russian, Turkish and other Navies.

Full particulars on Application.

London Office:
1 BILLITER BUILDINGS,
BILLITER ST.,
E.C.

G. & J. WEIR, LTD.
CATHCART,
GLASGOW.

Telegrams—
"GIWEIR, GLASGOW."
"HYDROKINETER, LONDON."

BENJ^{N.} GOODFELLOW,

ENGINEER, &C.

HYDE, NEAR MANCHESTER,

ENGLAND.

REFRIGERATING
AND
ICE MAKING
WITH
AMMONIA, CARBONIC ACID

OR OTHER GAS MACHINERY

Chilling and Cooling done on the Dry Air Principle, with Dry Air Machinery when required, also

HIGH-CLASS ENGINES
FOR
ELECTRIC LIGHTING,
BLOWING & VENTILATING
PURPOSES.

30ᴬ REDCROSS STREET, LIVERPOOL,
AND
ALBERT ROAD, SOUTHAMPTON.

Purveyors to the Royal Mail Steamers.

Telegraphic Address: "Thistle."

Mineral Waters.

J. Schweppe & Co. Ld.

Purveyors by Special Warrant of Appointment to the

QUEEN AND PRINCE OF WALES,

And (are Purveyors) to

The Pacific Steam Navigation Company.

Every Bottle of SCHWEPPE'S SODA WATER, LEMONADE, POTASS, SELTZER, &c., is protected by a Label bearing the "FOUNTAIN" TRADE MARK.

HEAD OFFICE·

51 Berners Street, London.

The HASLAM FOUNDRY & ENGINEERING CO. Ld.

INCORPORATED WITH

PONTIFEX & WOOD Ld.

Union Foundry, Derby, & 34 New Bridge St., London, E.C.

MANUFACTURERS OF

Refrigerating Machines

For use on board SHIP and on SHORE: for the COLD STORAGE of MEAT and all kinds of PERISHABLE FOOD.

These Machines are adopted by all the leading SHIPOWNERS and MEAT COMPANIES in all parts of the world.

Haslam's New Patent Cold Air Blast Machines

For chilling and freezing Meat.

Haslam's Patent Ice Plant.

Makers of Distilling Apparatus

FOR ALL KINDS OF SPIRITS.

BREWING PLANT.

MILK CONDENSING PLANT.

VINEGAR-MAKING PLANT.

TELEGRAMS:
"ZERO, DERBY." "PONFEX, LONDON."

Collard & Collard
METAL FRAME
GRAND PIANOS,
From 85 Guineas.

The New Metal Framed Trichord Grand Pianofortes by COLLARD and COLLARD, recently introduced, are of such compact dimensions as to render them suitable for rooms of very moderate dimensions. The most experienced judges are favorably attracted by the volume and quality of tone, added to a touch at once easy and responsive.

Collard & Collard
METAL FRAME
COTTAGE PIANOS,
From 45 Guineas.

These Pianofortes are not only world-renowned for their rich mellow tone and pure singing quality, but for depth and volume they are unsurpassed. Their capacity for remaining in tune, under trying conditions of climate, is another valuable and important feature.

COLLARD & COLLARD Pianos are displayed in great variety in the Warerooms of Pianoforte Dealers throughout Great Britain and the World.

⇢≋ESTABLISHED 1730.≋⇠

First Award, Chicago, 1893.

Gold Medal, Kimberley, 1892.

The Finest DRY GIN in the World.

J. & W. NICHOLSON & CO. Ltd.
DISTILLERIES :—CLERKENWELL & BROMLEY-BY-BOW, LONDON, ENGLAND.

ROCKLIFF BROTHERS Ltd.

EXPORT

AND

Manufacturing Stationers,

44 Castle Street,

LIVERPOOL.

CHADBURN & SON'S
PATENT "DUPLEX GONG" TELEGRAPHS.

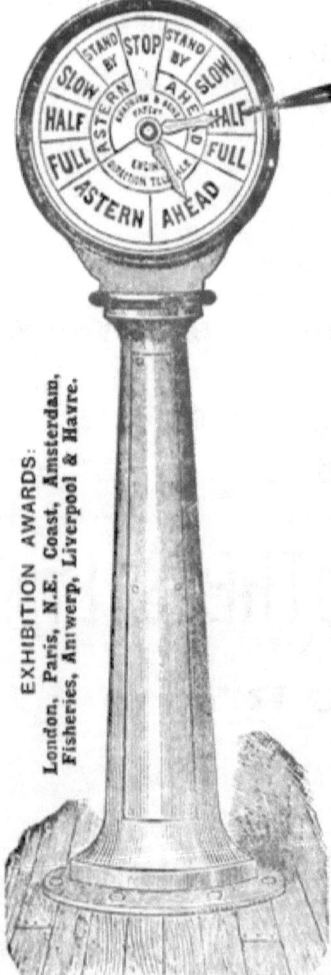

ENGINE TELEGRAPHS.
Duplex Gong { Deep Gong for Ahead. Shrill Gong for Astern.

Engine Automatic Direction Telltale.
Pointer shewing Engines Working Ahead or Astern.

Engine Revolution Speed Indicator
Shewing at a glance the Number of Revolutions per Minute.

STEERING TELEGRAPHS.
Duplex Gong { Deep Gong for Starboard Orders. Shrill Gong for Port   "

"LOOK-OUT" TELEGRAPH.
For Signalling between Forecastlehead and Bridge position of an Object Ahead or on Port or Starboard Bow.

DOCKING TELEGRAPHS,
For Warping Ship in and out of Dock.

ALARM GONGS,
SINGLE AND DUPLEX.

Admiralty Pattern Telegraphs.
Fitted with Machine-Cut Bevelled Wheels and Hollow Steel Shafting.

TORPEDO BOAT TELEGRAPHS,
Specially Constructed.

Telegraphs Fitted on Board 5000 Merchant Steamers, 350 Vessels of the British Navy, 350 Vessels of other Navies, including Her Majesty's new Battle Ships, Cruisers and Torpedo Destroyers; R.M.S. "Campania" and "Lucania"; Steamers of the Pacific Steam Navigation Company, Peninsular and Oriental, White Star, International, Royal Mail, Union, Donald Currie, North German Lloyds, &c. &c.   Steam Yachts, &c. &c.

Chadburn's Patent Engine Counters.

C. and Son's New Patent "Electric" Telegraphs for Ships.

Manufacturers and Adjusters of Ships' Compasses.

EXHIBITION AWARDS:
London, Paris, N.E. Coast, Amsterdam, Fisheries, Antwerp, Liverpool & Havre.

GLASGOW: 69 Anderston Quay.   NEWCASTLE-ON-TYNE: 83 Quayside.
LONDON: 105 Fenchurch Street.

OFFICE & WORKS:
TELEGRAPH WORKS, 11 Waterloo Road, LIVERPOOL.

HENRY WILSON & CO., LTD.
CORNHILL,
LIVERPOOL.

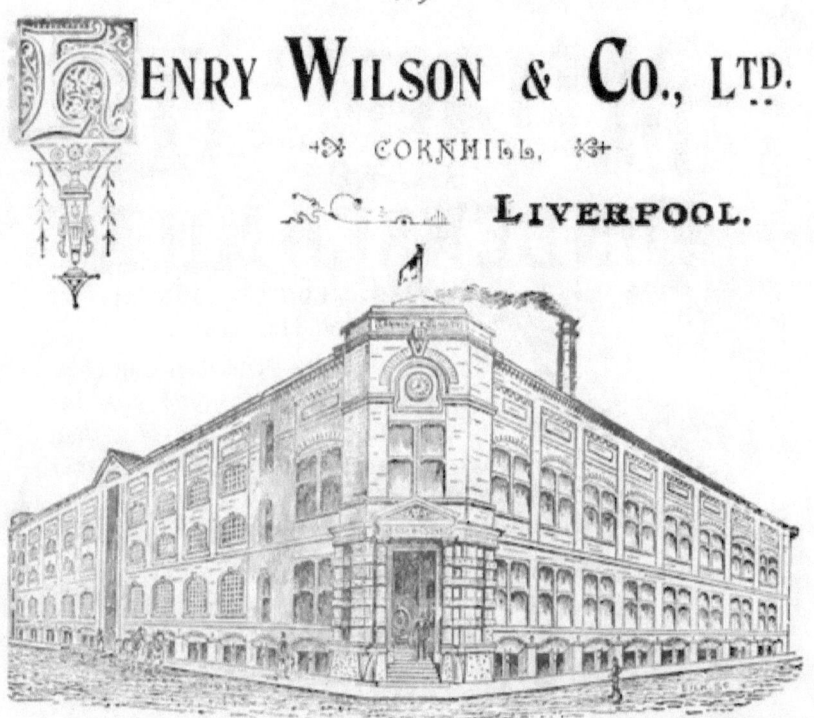

Iron and Brass Founders.

MANUFACTURERS AND EXPORTERS OF
EVERY DESCRIPTION OF HARDWARE.

SPECIALITY:
High-class Ships' Cooking Apparatus,

As supplied to Principal Steamship Lines, including

PACIFIC.
WHITE STAR.
CUNARD.
UNION,
PENINSULAR & ORIENTAL.
HAMBURG-AMERICAN.
CANADIAN PACIFIC RAILWAY CO.'S and
LEADING ENGLISH RAILWAY CO.'S Steamers.

Sole Makers of "ARGYRNAUT," the best White Metal for Ships' Fittings.

TELEGRAMS:—"WILSON, CORNHILL, LIVERPOOL."

MILKMAID BRAND CONDENSED MILK

The "BRITISH MEDICAL JOURNAL" of 27th July, 1895, says "According to the Report of our Commission, the 'MILKMAID' brand contains 990 PER CENT. MORE BUTTER-FAT than is contained, on an average, in the other brands examined. This is a fact of great importance to the public."

ANGLO-SWISS CONDENSED MILK CO.
10 MARK LANE, LONDON, E.C.

JOHN BROADWOOD & SONS,
(ESTABLISHED 1732,)
PIANOFORTE MAKERS
BY APPOINTMENT TO
HER MAJESTY THE QUEEN and all the ROYAL FAMILY.

PIANOS SPECIALLY MANUFACTURED FOR EXTREME CLIMATES.

SPECIAL FACILITIES FOR THE CONSTRUCTION OF ELABORATELY DECORATED PIANOS.

No. 1 — SHORT GRAND (Rosewood or Ebonized) 105 Guineas.

BROADWOODS,
33 GT. PULTENEY ST. (NEAR PICCADILLY CIRCUS),
LONDON W.

COOK & TOWNSHEND,

MANUFACTURERS,

SHIP & HOTEL FURNISHERS

AND

UPHOLSTERERS.

The Cheapest House for every description of Floor Covering, Furniture, Bedsteads, Bedding, Blankets, and every description of Household and Family Linen.

SPECIALITY FOR EXTRA COMFORT AT SEA—

DOWN QUILTS, PILLOWS & CUSHIONS.

BYROM ST. & DALE ST.
LIVERPOOL.

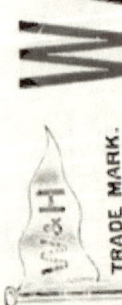
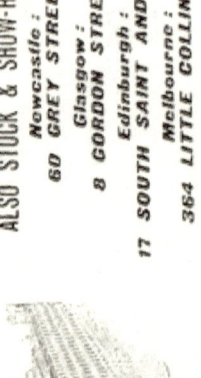

WALKER & HALL, ELECTRO WORKS, SHEFFIELD.

Electro Plate & Cutlery.

MANUFACTURERS OF STERLING SILVER GOODS OF EVERY DESCRIPTION.

MANUFACTURERS OF SHIPS' & HOTEL PLATE & ELECTRO PLATERS OF SHIPS' FITTINGS.

Manufacturers of the celebrated **FLAG BRAND** TRADE MARK.

ESTIMATES ON APPLICATION.

TELEGRAPHIC ADDRESS "BINGHAM, SHEFFIELD."

ALSO STOCK & SHOW-ROOMS
London:
45 HOLBORN VIADUCT.
Liverpool:
28 PARADISE STREET.
Manchester:
3 FOUNTAIN STREET.
Cardiff:
89 ST. MARY STREET.

ALSO STOCK & SHOW-ROOMS
Newcastle:
60 GREY STREET.
Glasgow:
8 GORDON STREET.
Edinburgh:
17 SOUTH SAINT ANDREW ST.
Melbourne:
364 LITTLE COLLINS ST.

Electro Works, 1891.

Mitchell's CASTOR OIL.

Guaranteed pure cold drawn, and absolutely free from any nauseous taste.

THE LANCET of 8th June, 1895, says—"MITCHELL'S PROCESS of extracting and refining Castor Oil is obviously an improvement which the profession cannot fail to approve and welcome, since in removing the great objection to the oil, namely, that of repulsive taste, as well as in securing its full therapeutic effect, it is calculated to assist and to facilitate the administration of a very valuable therapeutic agent."

THE PHARMACEUTICAL JOURNAL of 11th May, 1895, says—"The oil expressed by this process is absolutely cold drawn . . . and in all its stages of manufacture has a simple bland taste resembling olive or almond oil, in marked contrast to the nauseous taste usually associated with it." . . . . .

THE FAMILY DOCTOR of 6th July, 1895, says—" . . . The taste is simply pleasantly nutty . . . another advantage which the oil manufactured by MITCHELL'S PROCESS possesses is that only half the ordinary dose is necessary on account of its purity. We have a very high opinion of this cold-drawn Castor Oil, and recommend it with confidence to nurses, mothers, and other household authorities."

THE COURT CIRCULAR of 8th June, 1895, says—" . . . The various Medical Journals are equally laudatory in their good opinions, and when the value of this remedial agent is remembered, and the fact that what was previously nauseating is now rendered palatable, it is no exaggeration to say that Mr. MITCHELL by his invention, has conferred a blessing on humanity."

A dose of this Oil consists of only half the quantity of ordinary Castor Oil.

TO BE HAD FROM ALL CHEMISTS, DRUGGISTS AND STORES THROUGHOUT THE WORLD.

In Bottles, at 6d, 9d and 1/-.

ELKINGTON & CO. LTD.
CHURCH STREET.
~ Liverpool. ~

 Goldsmiths and Silversmiths by Appointment to Her Majesty the Queen & Royal Family.

ORIGINAL PATENTEES OF

ELKINGTON ELECTRO-PLATE.

ESTABLISHED HALF A CENTURY.

PATTERN BOOKS of Designs of Silver Testimonial and other Plate on application.

Clubs, Steam-Ship Companies and Merchants supplied with their Celebrated Elkington Plate at Special Rates.

Telephone No. 5239.

J. W. RAY & CO.

ENGINE & STEERING
TELEGRAPH MAKERS,

Makers of THREE DIAL TELEGRAPHS, AUTOMATIC ENGINE REPLIES, and SCREENED BLACK DIALS,

PATENTED IN UNITED KINGDOM, GERMANY, AND U.S.A.

COMPASS ADJUSTERS,
NAUTICAL INSTRUMENT MAKERS,

BRASS-FOUNDERS AND ELECTRICIANS,

(Special Staff of experienced Electricians attend to Electric Light and Bell Repairs on board Ship.)

---

8 CANNING PLACE, LIVERPOOL,

(OPPOSITE NORTH END CUSTOM HOUSE.)

WORKS Cooper's Row.   **FOUNDRY** 37 Mersey Street.

Our Telegraphs have been adopted in the latest vessels of the following firms:—

Pacific Steam Navigation Company.
White Star Line.
Union Line.
Hamburg American Line.
Woermann Line.
Warren Line.
Deutsche Ost African Line.

Asiatic Steam Navigation Company.
African Steamship Company.
Atlantic Transport Line.
Harrison Line.
Bibby Line.
Bates' Line.
Johnston Line, &c. &c.

IHLERS & BELL,
LIVERPOOL,
EXPORT BOTTLERS OF

BASS' INDIA PALE ALE
AND
GUINNESS' Foreign Extra STOUT,
"BULL BRAND."

Sole Export Bottling Agents for

GUILD & CO.'S (Inverness) PALE ALE.

ESTABLISHED IN 1834.

George Angus & Company, Ltd.

Contractors to the Admiralty,
Home, Foreign & Colonial Governments,
St. John's Works,
NEWCASTLE=ON=TYNE.

SPECIALITIES IN

SINGLE AND DOUBLE LEATHER BELTING, SPECIAL LEATHER LINK BELTS, for Main Drives, Dynamos, &c.

HELVETIA AND RAW HIDE BELTING.

INDIA RUBBER, COTTON AND HAIR BELTING, Endless Belts of all kinds for Agricultural Purposes.

LEATHER, RUBBER AND CANVAS FIRE HOSE.

FIRE BRIGADE FITTINGS of every description, **INDIA RUBBER SHEETS, VALVES, WASHERS, BUFFERS,** &c.

EVERY DESCRIPTION OF LEATHER AND INDIA RUBBER FOR GENERAL MECHANICAL PURPOSES.

SPECIAL TERMS TO EXPORTERS.

WAREHOUSES:
PRINCES BUILDINGS, DALE STREET, LIVERPOOL,
ALSO AT
LONDON, LEEDS, MANCHESTER & CARDIFF.

LLOYD & LLOYD,

Manufacturers and Patentees of

Wrought Iron & Steel Tubes

FOR ALL PURPOSES.

BOILER TUBES AND ACCESSORIES IN IRON, STEEL AND HOMOGENEOUS METAL.

Tubes and Fittings for Water, Steam, Gas, Air, Chemicals, &c. Coils.

ELECTRICALLY WELDED SPECIALITIES.

LAP-WELDED TUBES UP TO FOUR FEET IN DIAMETER.

BIRMINGHAM {ALBION TUBE WORKS,
{COOMBS' WOOD TUBE WORKS, HALESOWEN.
LONDON, 90 CANNON STREET, E.C.
LIVERPOOL, 63 PARADISE STREET.
MANCHESTER, 42 DEANSGATE.
&c.

PACIFIC LINE.

The Pacific Steam Navigation Co. issue Tickets for the undermentioned Tours:—

Round SOUTH AMERICA, in connection with all Atlantic Lines, both between Europe and North America.

To SAN FRANCISCO (via Chile and Peru), Overland from San Francisco to United States and back to Europe by the White Star Line.

To SAN FRANCISCO (via Chile and Peru), from San Francisco to Australia and New Zealand and back to Europe from Australia by the Orient Line.

To SPAIN.—Outwards to Gibraltar by Orient Line, and home from Lisbon, Vigo, Corunna or La Pallice (La Rochelle).

31 JAMES STREET,
LIVERPOOL.

"THE ACADÉMIE DE MÉDECINE OF FRANCE
HAS PLACED

Apollinaris

("THE QUEEN OF TABLE WATERS")

At the **HEAD** of **ALL** the Waters examined for **PURITY & FREEDOM** from Disease Germs."

SOLE IMPORTERS:

THE APOLLINARIS CO. Ltd.
4 STRATFORD PLACE, OXFORD ST., LONDON, W

THIS BOOK IS DUE ON THE LAST DATE STAMPED BELOW

AN INITIAL FINE OF 25 CENTS
WILL BE ASSESSED FOR FAILURE TO RETURN THIS BOOK ON THE DATE DUE. THE PENALTY WILL INCREASE TO 50 CENTS ON THE FOURTH DAY AND TO $1.00 ON THE SEVENTH DAY OVERDUE.

OCT 23 1939
1939
FEB 18 1978

FEB 19 1941 M

27Apr'50WZ

27Oct'52HD
OCT 13 1957

FEB 15 1966 5

REC'D LD
FEB 7'66 -7 PM

SEP 3 1976
SOC. CIR. AP 2 '78

LD 21-100m-7,'39(402s)

THE UNIVERSITY OF CALIFORNIA LIBRARY

www.ingramcontent.com/pod-product-compliance
Lightning Source LLC
Chambersburg PA
CBHW021352230426
43666CB00006B/493